EXMOOR'S
Greatest Walk

To Sunya

EXMOOR'S
Greatest Walk

Alastair Brian Atkin

Illustrated by the Author

EXMOOR BOOKS
in association with
Exmoor Tourist Association

First published in 2000 by Exmoor Books
Copyright © 2000 A.B. Atkin

ISBN 0 86183 406 2

British Library Cataloguing-in-Publication-Data
A CIP data for this book is available from the British Library

EXMOOR BOOKS
Dulverton, Somerset

Exmoor Books is a partnership between
The Exmoor Press and The Exmoor National Park Authority.
The views expressed in this book are those of the author and not necessarily
those of the publisher or the Exmoor National Park Authority.

Trade sales enquiries
HALSGROVE
Halsgrove House
Lower Moor Way
Tiverton EX16 6SS
T: 01884 243242
F: 01884 243325
www.halsgrove.com

Printed and bound in Great Britain
by MPG Ltd, Bodmin.

CONTENTS

FOREWORD

The Exmoor Tourist Association is delighted to be associated with *Exmoor's Greatest Walk*, Brian Atkin's second publication with Exmoor Books. Brian Atkin has been a very loyal and influential supporter of Exmoor and its tourism industry. Over the past few years he has succeeded in increasing the profile of Exmoor as a popular destination for walkers.

What we find so attractive about this particular walk is its emphasis on public transport. Visitors can travel to Exmoor by car (or by public transport) and then enjoy a most rewarding holiday without needing to use their car again. Brian shares our love of Exmoor and this is very evident from this book. However, he is also concerned that this is an environmentally sensitive area and any use by visitors must respect this.

Brian has also been a great supporter of the Exmoor Paths Partnership. The Paths Partnership works closely with the tourism industry on Exmoor to improve and protect the many pathways that traverse Exmoor. The partnership aims to persuade visitors to Exmoor to help pay for the maintenance and improvement of the paths and walkways. This initiative called 'visitor payback' is already supported by nearly one hundred businesses on Exmoor and is part of a new partnership between the National Park Authority, the tourism industry and visitors to Exmoor.

Exmoor has been described as England's greatest secret. With the help of publications like this we hope that more people will be persuaded to venture onto Exmoor for the first time. We are certain that once they have they will join the many thousands who are convinced that this is the most beautiful and romantic place in England.

Malcolm Higgins
Exmoor Tourist Association

INTRODUCTION

This book has evolved out of my long love affair with Exmoor. Having enjoyed the unique pleasures of this small region for many years I now wanted to share them with others. In recent times this desire has evolved into an amble through many of my favourite places. Thus the book is a personal account of the beauty, points of interest and history along the route, together with some practical advice for those wishing to follow my steps. Intended as an easy-paced exploration, it can be based on two holiday centres during summer months.

My first long walks grew out of a yearning for wild places. In part this came from an increasing dislike for the Lincolnshire of my teens, a man-made land of large flat intensively cultivated fields, with few trees and lack of grass, and which was defined by straight roads, banks, dykes and drains.

During those and later years I sought the sparsely populated untamed hills of England and it was not long before my steps led me to Exmoor. At first I wanted to believe that these new regions had always been wild but eventually had to accept that this was not so. Man has been around for a long time in this part of Europe and almost all its flora, fauna and physical features have been modified by him to a greater or lesser extent. This realisation brought no diminution in attraction of these lonely places and led to an added fascination in the people who had been there before me.

Exmoor is marginal land at the fringes of colonisation where the tides of humanity have flowed and ebbed over the millennia. In the following pages it will become apparent that my route around this little region is as much a trek through past peoples as through present day beautiful scenes. Elsewhere historic evidence may have been swept away by many later arrivals but here the past has a habit of lingering on.

It is sometimes claimed that Exmoor is a place where time stands still but this is not so. Exmoor time, freed from the constraints of modern society, tends to slip away almost unnoticed.

Exmoor defies succinct description. However the ground provides a starting point as the rocks of all areas define their basic structures. Exmoor's are mostly ancient Devonian, formed from mud and sand deposited on the bed of a primaeval ocean some 350 million years ago when, of all places, it was located in the southern tropics. Later upheavals forced up the earth's crust, tilting and compressing the strata to form the rocks which now underlie the area. The mountains formed then have long since been worn down to the gentle hills which now characterise much of the inland scene. The coast is very different and often rugged, the result of both the scouring action of frost and ice during the Ice Ages and erosion by water in both recent and distant times.

The region is not a single block of upland but areas of high ground divided by beautiful winding river valleys. It also tilts from the north, so the north flowing watercourses are steep and dramatic and those heading south more gentle and serene.

Changes in climate are also responsible for some marked scene changes, the moorland tops being very different from nearby valley bottoms. It does not take a walker very long or very far to stride away from pretty flower gardens of attractive villages to wet windswept moorland tops where only the most hardy grasses and heather survive.

From the foregoing it will be apparent that Exmoor's attraction lies in its wide variety of scene in a very small compass. A walk through its constantly changing landscapes may give the impression of an extensive region but in reality Exmoor National Park only covers 267 square miles.

On my first visit to Exmoor in 1951 I walked from Dunster to Combe Martin via Selworthy, Minehead, Porlock and Lynmouth. The National Park did not then exist and the rarely used footpaths of the time were often obscure, in marked contrast to today's well signposted and maintained ways. On the second day I managed to reach Culbone along the coast but after this was obliged to retreat to the main coastal highway. The traffic of the time was light and on the way to Countisbury the road passed through lovely heather moorland, much of which, alas, has since been lost. Two unforgettable days were spent exploring the hills, valleys and coast around Lynmouth before again encountering serious path problems between the Heddon Valley and Combe Martin.

Although Exmoor had made a lasting impression I did not return until the late 1970s. After this visits became frequent. In the early 1980s my youngest son and I made an anticlockwise walk around the region. As always the coast was magnificent but some of the later marches across high farmland proved disappointing because inland Exmoor is a shy countryside, hiding its best from those who are not yet its intimates.

It was not until 1992 that I again attempted another circular walk. This was a clockwise trek across the high ground from Dunkery Beacon to Chapman Barrows and then back along the coast. For much of the way the weather was atrocious and my outstanding memory is of a challenging but very rewarding journey across high lonely hills and cliffs.

The experiences of many years have now been distilled into the present walk. The book is in two sections. The first and major part is a detailed description of the lovely scenes, points of interest and my past experiences along the way. The second gives practical advice for those who might wish to follow the route.

Although the walk passes through every type of Exmoor scene, a number of my favourite places are omitted because the alternative would have led to extensive zig zags and an overlong walk length. The final outcome is one hundred miles, split into ten or more stages. The walk is intended to be a leisurely exploration but can also provide an energetic challenge. A start can be made anywhere on the route but the description is based on Minehead, the most accessible point.

I should point out that the first part of the walk lies outside the bounds of the National Park. This area of West Somerset is not only beautiful and full of interest but also provides a marked contrast to the very different scenes which follow.

Exmoor has extensive holiday accommodation but this is more limited in remote areas. Although overnight stops can be made at the end of each stage, available public transport during the summer months makes it possible to base most of the walk on a combination of accommodation at Minehead and Lynmouth/Lynton. Alternatively the walk can provide two undemanding walking holidays, one based at Minehead covering the eastern half of the walk and the other at Lynmouth/Lynton to complete the whole. It is advisable to book all overnight accommodation before commencing the walk. Short cuts and other alternatives to suit individual tastes are also suggested.

The OS Outdoor Leisure Map No. 9, Exmoor, is highly recommended for wayfinding. Detailed route descriptions, grid references for key turning points and other useful advice are given in the second part of the book.

The weather is always important. It is a truism that the British Isles do not have a climate, only weather. Its extremes can make the same walk anything between a great pleasure and an exhausting experience. In addition one type of weather can quickly follow another and conditions at the top of a high hill are always very different from those at its bottom. Therefore a close check on local weather forecasts is highly recommended. The present walk crosses both exposed high moors and tall sections of the coast and where feasible wild weather alternatives are suggested.

I hope that readers will learn something of interest about this unusual and relatively unknown corner of England and that those who go on to follow my footsteps will have every bit as much enjoyment as I have along the way.

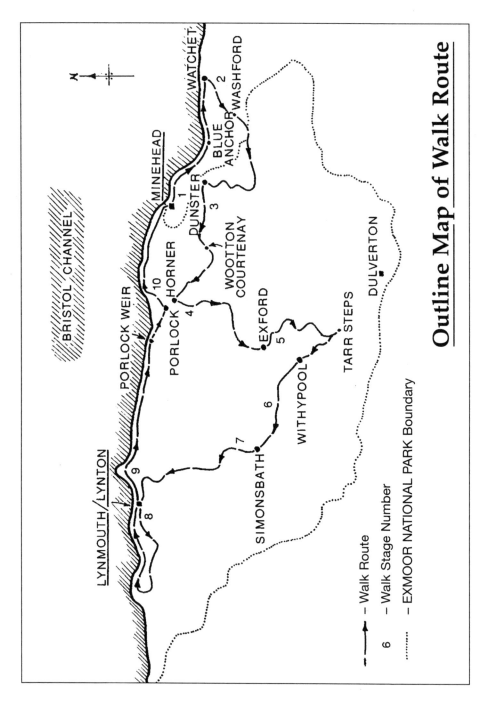

Outline Map of Walk Route

N

BRISTOL CHANNEL

WATCHET
WASHFORD
BLUE ANCHOR
MINEHEAD
DUNSTER
WOOTTON COURTENAY
HORNER
PORLOCK WEIR
PORLOCK
EXFORD
DULVERTON
TARR STEPS
WITHYPOOL
SIMONSBATH
LYNMOUTH/LYNTON

1
2
3
4
5
6
7
8
9
10

— Walk Route
6 — Walk Stage Number
.... — EXMOOR NATIONAL PARK Boundary

⤜ STAGE 1 ⤛

MINEHEAD TO WATCHET

This stage provides an undemanding start to the walk around Exmoor because there are only gentle hills along the West Somerset coast between Minehead and the old port of Watchet.

The start of every long distance walk is always the same. The earlier happy anticipation is swept away by a sudden lack of confidence and reluctance to begin. Now the undertaking seems foolhardy in the extreme. However once a steady stride has been established all concerns and discomforts are swept away, replaced by present pleasure and anticipation of much more to come.

On leaving the shops on Minehead's Avenue behind, the route turns right at the Esplanade. The sandy strand is now divided by long stone groynes, part of the town's new sea defences, and it may be expedient to continue eastwards along the promenade. Fortunately the large garish holiday camp on the right is both the first and last along the way. At the end of the Esplanade a public footpath starts beside the golf club house and leads onto a shingle bank. From here an uninterrupted sandy-stony shore extends eastwards for several miles.

The new unspoilt scene is wide and lovely. The Bristol Channel has the second highest tidal range in the world, exceeded only by that of the Bay of Fundy in Canada. Sometimes the salt water wets the foot of the shingle bank above the shore and at others is glimpsed far away across sandy-stony flats. Winds roam free across these empty spaces and so does the sand when dry, its streaming eddies stinging any exposed human legs. Usually the shore is wide enough for walking and this way is preferable because it encourages total absorption in the seascape. The alternative, a public footpath on the top of the sea bank, is both stony underfoot and subject to distraction from activity on the adjacent golf course.

This low lying coast and wide beach may lie outside the official boundary of Exmoor National Park but they provide a most attractive contrast to the more typical Exmoor scenes which follow. For me this place also evokes fond memories of a long stretch of lighter hued sand on England's east coast where, during the inter-war years, I grew up and first became a walker. However the present scene displays a marked difference to the one in the east. Here the dominating horizontals of shore and sea do not reach out to seeming infinity but to distant Welsh hills and others far and near along the Somerset coast.

Ker Moor Beach

Beyond Warren Point the buildings of Minehead and even the towering bulk of Beacon Hill, marking the end of Exmoor's high coast, drop out of sight behind the nearby shingle bank. Ahead the long line of chalets facing the sea were built during the inter-war seaside holiday boom and still provide quiet holidays for those who come here year after year. Out of sight behind the chalets, screened by trees and bushes, there is a stretch of water known as the Hawn which may be the surviving remnant of Dunster's once busy ship haven. The chalets end at a car park. Beyond this a straight concrete-lined overflow channel reaches the beach. It was constructed to alleviate the former flooding of low lying parts of Dunster. In summer months the bed of this channel is often as dry as a bone but when winter comes so do the floods, pouring out onto the beach in torrents of white water. At these times a footbridge a short distance inland provides a safe and dry crossing.

With a new wider inland view, the puny sea bank seems poor protection for the low lying meadows behind. Further away higher arable fields lead up to darker wooded hills. Across the sea on clear days a long panorama of the Welsh coast is topped by the distant Brecon Beacons. In the middle of the water the low island of Flat Holm may shyly play hide and seek but its lofty companion. Steep Holm, always stands proud and preening.

On first sighting from the Quantock ridge in 1951, I mistook Steep Holm for Lundy. My knowledge of the region was then limited! Many years were to pass before I set foot on this fascinating, nowadays uninhabited, limestone rock set in the middle of a sea surrounded by land visibly occupied by man. Over the years the island has had many inhabitants, both warlike and peaceful. Around the time of the first millenium the Danes were using it as a secure base for their ravaging raids on the surrounding coasts and in the Middle Ages a a small priory here housed a group of monks. In the nineteenth century it was heavily fortified with cannons to protect the hinterland of the Bristol Channel from a feared French invasion and in World War Two with breech loading guns to deter the Germans. The nineteenth century soldiers lived in solid well constructed barracks, now the visitor centre, but their twentieth century counterparts had only flimsy huts which have all but disintegrated. The substantial Victorian gun emplacements and their less robust twentieth century equivalents are scattered all over the island. However these are not the outstanding feature of the place.

That honour must surely belong to the pervasive jungle of tall alexanders, first introduced by the monks as a vegetable but now grown rampant.

Scandinavian place names are rare in the West but were familiar to me in my youth. Consequently they remind me of home and I always look out for them. On my first visit I was particularly struck by the Danish word 'holm' embodied in the name of these two islands.

Steep Holm is best explored on day trips from Weston-super-Mare and the pleasure vessels *Waverley* and *Balmoral* call in occasionally. For those satisfied with a distant view it provides a compulsive focal point for the eye, though often appearing in an unexpected quarter.

Progress along the sand and shingle brings the West Somerset Railway ever closer and the rails and shore finally meet at Blue Anchor Station. Although the name has been around for some time, much of the settlement is modern. Here a small stream known as the Pill once meandered through marshy ground down to the shore.

This word, common in both Wales and Cornwall, is a corruption of the Celtic 'Pwll' meaning 'Pool'. Although place names in Somerset are predominantly Anglo-Saxon, Celtic ones still persist, the most obvious being 'combe', the almost universal word for a small valley.

Nowadays the seaward end of the present valley is separated from the shore by a concrete embankment with the coast road along its top. The original pool has gone and much of the former marsh is now drained and occupied by holiday caravans. In addition to the railway station there are several cafes and a more venerable pub at the eastern end of the embankment.

The name 'Blue Anchor' is said to have originated in the days when inland roads were poor and much of the area's trade was carried by a host of small topsail schooners, luggers and barques, each carrying a cargo of between 30 and a 100 tons. When becalmed these vessels often waited offshore because the sea bed here provided a firm anchorage. Later when the wind returned and the ships' anchors were hauled up, these emerged from the water coated with a blue-grey lias mud which originated from the cliffs to the east. Since that time, in much the same way as the mud to the anchors, the name has stuck to the place.

At the point where the road turns uphill and away from the coast, there is a choice of ways forward. One follows the stony rocky shore to Watchet and the other passes along the top of the cliffs. The first of these traverses a magnificent wilderness like a surreal lost world.

Looking back at distant Minehead from Blue Anchor beach

From here the only signs of humanity are in faraway Wales or back along the coast at now distant Minehead. The cliffs looming above are composed of layers of grey-blue lias interspersed with strips of white or pink alabaster. In some parts the rock layers have remained horizontal, as originally laid down long ago in the bed of a former sea, but elsewhere they are buckled by earth movements into contorted shapes. The alabaster was once used to make ornaments and suitable loose stones from the shore still provide attractive paperweights.

Below the cliffs there are extensive rock platforms, often eroded by the sea into grotesque shapes. At low tide there are often strange sounds of escaping gas. Fossils, mostly ammonites and an ancient form of mussel, are found in these rocks. While one of these creatures has disappeared from the face of the earth, the other has survived apparently unchanged. Together they underline the stark fact that man is a brash newcomer on the scene. The best area for fossil hunting is the bed of loose stones at the west end of Warren Bay but much patience is needed for success.

High tides wash the base of the cliffs along the 2 miles stretch between Blue Anchor and Watchet and there is only one escape point at Warren Bay. This route should only be attempted when the tide is on the ebb and tide times should always be checked beforehand. The walking surface changes constantly and is often rough and very slippery. Continual care is needed and beach sandals are definitely not suitable footwear.

The cliff top alternative is attractive for quite different reasons but also has its own drawback. Between Blue Anchor Bay and the the start of lias cliffs there is a short stretch of soft red sandstone. In recent times part of the cliff path in this sector was lost and has been replaced by a detour. In order to re-join the remainder of the cliff top path to Watchet it is now necessary to walk eastwards up the road for half a mile before turning left through trees down to the coast. The relatively narrow road up to this point has no footway and is both unpleasant and potentially dangerous for pedestrians when traffic is heavy during the summer months.

On leaving the road the new leafy surroundings bring immediate peace and relief. The enclosing thick foliage of summer months may limit distant views but there are glimpses of nearby arable fields, usually bearing cereals.

Ordinarily these crops would be of no particular interest but here they provide one of the walk's main contrasts. Along many miles ahead the way will cross uplands where the ground is poor, high and exposed, permitting only hill farming or none at all. The present arable fields continue beside the path to Watchet and for a short distance beyond.

At length the diverted route turns right onto the old cliff top path. In medieval times a popular pilgrimage place stood in the vicinity. This chapel, dedicated to Our Lady, has long since been lost to the sea. No obvious trace now remains but there are reports of dressed stones being found nearby. The prime object of veneration was said to have been a statue of the Virgin which hovered in a perilous position above the sea for a very long time. However the old pilgrims' route to the site still exists. Starting from Cleeve Abbey, two miles inland, it passes through Washford, Old Cleeve and Chapel Cleeve on the way. In one place, and possibly two, the stone steps provided for the pious wayfarers still survive. The next stage, from Watchet to Dunster, approaches Cleeve Abbey and there will be an opportunity to visit the site.

Nature in the form of the sea may have destroyed a man-made sanctuary but she has replaced it with one of her own. The waves constantly fret the relatively soft rocks of the cliffs in this vicinity and in the past one section of high ground beside the path slumped before coming to rest half way to the shore. Now detached from both the coast below and the ground above, this shelf has become a delightful lush wildlife sanctuary where no men go.

At length the path emerges from trees to pass along the edge of arable fields on top of the foliage covered cliff. In addition to inland and sea views there are now occasional sightings of the rugged shore below. I have passed this way many times but on one occasion, when the day was very hot and the nearby corn nearly ripened, the shimmering heat rising from the crop so softened the appearance of the wilder harsher distant hills that for once they could only display an unusual benevolence.

Arrival at Warren Bay is signalled by a drop in height and a view of holiday caravans. There is access to the shore here but the cliff top path continues upwards along the edge of a camp site to the top of the hill which stands to the west of Watchet. Nowadays known as Daw's Castle, this high place has traces of old earthworks. These are a remnant of much more extensive remains now lost to the sea. This hill was Watchet's place of refuge in earlier unsettled times and may even have been a former site of the town. Sketchy evidence suggests that there was a place of worship up here and that it may have been the parish church before the present one was built further inland. Watchet is very old but only entered written history in Anglo-Saxon times with reports of Danish raids in both AD 914 and AD 988. Predictably silver coins made in the mint at Watchet have appeared in Scandinavian museums. The millennium of the second raid in 1988 provided the inhabitants of the town with an opportunity for some splendid celebrations which will be long remembered.

Daw's Castle panorama ranges from the town and sea at its foot to the tamed Brendon Hills away to the south and the more distant rolling empty spaces and deep nooks of the Quantocks to the southeast. The oldest part of the town is situated in the narrow valley bottom close to the harbour. In former times both sides of this harbour had sheltering headlands but these are now eroded away. The northern part of the town has become increasingly vulnerable to the sea and recently an extensive concrete sea wall was constructed to provide a measure of protection.

Today the only significant structure on Daw's Castle is a disused lime kiln and a stile nearby gives access to the coast road. This narrow highway has no footway and can be unpleasant for pedestrians when traffic is heavy. However there is another footpath 100 yards on the right which passes through fields down to the inland edge of Watchet. Here the former Mineral Railway once left the town on its way into the hills and an adjacent steel bridge still carries the surviving West Somerset Railway towards Minehead. At the bottom of the hill the walk turns left to the town centre along the road known as Whitehall. Some local wags would have visitors believe that the more famous Whitehall takes its name from this one. Along the way one of the new houses built on the site of the former Mineral Railway is called 'Esperanza' after one the former steam locomotives which plied up and down the line. Earlier this engine had hauled passenger trains around the oldest underground railway in the world, London's Circle Line. The arrival of electric trains at the turn of the twentieth century must have come as a great relief to travellers. Even today the tunnels remain encrusted by the soot laid down all those years ago.

All the local towns have had their ups and downs and Watchet is no exception. Its period of greatest prosperity came in the late nineteenth century when the high grade iron ore mined in the Brendon Hills was shipped out of the port to the steelworks in South Wales. These hills, some 8 miles inland, rise to a height of 1200 feet and their high grade ore was essential for the then new

Watchet Harbour

Bessemer steel-making process. The mineral line provided an efficient means of transport to the coast and simultaneously the harbour was extended and equipped with loading hoists. Many of the town's buildings date from this period. However the most striking reminder is not here but six miles away in the Brendon Hills where a long steep incline carried the railway from the plateau top down into the valley. The trucks were moved along the incline by cable from a winding house located at the top. Although disused for nearly a century, much of the line's route can still be traced and work is at present underway to preserve the overgrown incline as a fitting monument to the initiative and drive of those entrepreneurial times.

After many centuries of use the harbour's commercial traffic finally came to an end a few years ago when the local shipping line went out of business. Until then the sight of large cargo vessels passing through the narrow entrance in all weathers provided endless fascination for bystanders. Now only small craft and occasional larger pleasure vessels come and go. When open, the small museum in Market Street provides an excellent insight to the town's long and special history.

Although Watchet has several claims to fame there is one which is unique. A century ago there was growing recognition that the traditional songs and dances of this country were becoming lost. The social upheaval caused by the industrial revolution and the consequent movement of the nation's population into manufacturing towns and cities had been the prime cause. The urgent search for native rural music, often honed to great beauty through centuries of performance, came just in the nick of time because by then many of the surviving singers and musicians were very old.

Watchet played an key role in this activity. Collectors searching for old sea songs, having met with little success in the country's larger ports, began to turn their attention to the older smaller ones. Thus the doyen folk song and dance collector, Cecil Sharp, who travelled around the countryside on his bicycle, came to Watchet and here on the quay he met John Short.

This old seaman had travelled the world as a deck hand on sailing ships and in the process acquired the nickname 'Yankee Jack' from the time he served on ships attempting to break the Union blockade of Confederate sea ports during the American Civil War. From this old seaman Cecil Sharp obtained the most comprehensive collection of English and American sea songs ever recorded, including both *Rio Grande* and *Shenandoah*. By all accounts John Short was a simple God fearing man who never aspired to be anything other than a serving seaman. It is said that he had a rich, powerful and resonant voice which would have been the envy of many professional singers and that he sang lustily in the local Baptist chapel until a short time before his death in 1933. His old cottage on Market Street has an appropriate commemorative plaque.

Watchet has cafés, restaurants, shops and accommodation. For the walker using Minehead as a base there is a good bus service back to the larger town and also trains for most of the year.

A corner of Watchet Harbour

⇥ STAGE 2 ⇤

FROM WATCHET TO DUNSTER

Watchet is the easterly point of the walk. From here it heads south-west and then west into Exmoor National Park before climbing the first high hill on the way to Dunster.

Watchet's main thoroughfare, Swain Street, formerly known by the less salubrious name of Swine Street, heads away from the harbour. Beyond the railway bridge there is a tarmac path on the right. The lorry park in the narrow valley bottom below is followed by a large paper mill, the main industry of the town. This substantial works developed from a small water-driven mill beside the stream. Ahead a brick industrial chimney, now disused, stands against the sky. It was erected after the paper mill had switched from water power to steam. The flue from the steam boiler was constructed up the side of the hill and into this stack to maximise draft for the fire below.

St Decuman's church tower is the next and more pleasing lofty object. Watchet parish church is named after a man who has a small but special niche in Christian history. Decuman was a member of the large group of Celtic missionaries, mostly originating from Wales, who converted the heathen South West to Christianity during the Dark Ages. Tradition has it that he set out to sea from Wales on a hurdle(!) together with his cow to supply fresh milk. The object of this uncertain voyage was to convert the natives of his eventual landing place to Christianity. A combination of winds, currents and tides finally cast him safely ashore at Watchet and he immediately set about his missionary work. This proved difficult because the local Anglo-Saxons, who probably still preferred their Nordic gods, objected to his efforts. The legend then states that one of them was so incensed that he chopped off Decuman's head.

This might well have been the end of the story but Decuman picked his head up, washed it carefully in a nearby spring and placed it back on his neck. Legend goes on to say that he then continued with his missionary work, no doubt with more success than before.

A tangible connection with this story can be found below the church. Here some roughly formed steps lead down to a spot where clear running water emerges from the ground and runs through two stone basins in turn. This is St Decuman's Well.

There will be other encounters with Celtic saints along the way. They presumably spoke a different language to the majority of the local inhabitants

St Decuman's Well, Watchet

and their church was later absorbed into that of Rome but remarkably fifteen hundred years later their names and sometimes their stories have survived.

As mentioned earlier, present day St Decuman's church may not have been the original parish church of Watchet and the fact that no part of its structure is older than the fourteenth century supports this theory.

In more recent times the churchyard gained fictional fame as the place where the wedding guest was accosted by Coleridge's Ancient Mariner and then obliged to listen to the latter's bleak turgid tale. Poets Coleridge and Wordsworth had been attracted to this coast by its remote romantic beauty and lived for a while at nearby Nether Stowey. However their outlandish behaviour, especially during long walks, disturbed the local countryfolk who, as those were Napoleonic War times, thought they might be French spies. An official investigation cleared the two but led to the end of their poetry partnership in this part of the world. Incidently the poem's description of the embarkation port fits the Watchet scene but the word 'kirk' does not belong here.

From the church the path descends to the valley bottom. After passing Snailholt Farm, now a house, it crosses a meadow heading for Kentsford Farm, formerly a manor. In the short distance from the start of the stage a revived beheaded missionary and a sombre loquacious mariner have both been encountered and there is more to come.

Four hundred years ago a lady clad in funeral vestments carrying a lantern came by dead of night along this very path. She was Florence Wyndham of Kentsford Manor. On being taken ill she had lapsed into a deep coma and was thought to have died. As her body was being placed in the Wyndham family vault in St Decuman's church, a greedy sexton observed her rings and decided to get them for himself. During the night he returned to the vault with a lantern but being unable to prise the jewellery off her stiff fingers, started to cut them away with his knife. Then, horrified, he saw flowing blood and the body beginning to stir with pain. In terror he charged away leaving his lamp behind.

The lady arose, picked up the sexton's lantern and then made her way along the present path to her home. On arrival she had to beat on the door for long time before convincing her husband that she was alive and not a spirit. However all's well that ends well and she later gave birth to a son, from whom all subsequent Wyndhams are said to have descended. This grizzly tale, containing both a moral and a happy ending, would have been recounted to many generations of local youngsters in the old dim lights of dark cold winter nights.

At Kentsford the house and oldest farm buildings display their medieval origins. The way goes through the yard and over the stream before heading up a track to a gate where there were once two railways. One survives as the West Somerset Railway and the other, the former Mineral Line, is now a pleasant hedge-enclosed path with the ballast which once supported its rails providing a firm walking surface. The route turns left along this path. In contemporary gravestone language, 'a melancholy accident' once took place here. Due to inadequate signalling procedures two steam engines travelling in opposite directions crashed head-on with fatal results.

A glimpse of Kentsford Manor

By now the narrow valley at Watchet has broadened out into a wide reach of pleasant meadows bounded by hedgerows and trees. Apart from occasional passing trains this is a very peaceful place. At one point the river flowing down towards the sea meanders close to the old line, adding the sound of ripples to other more muted sounds of the countryside.

Eventually the low embankment of the original line curves away to the left and the path continues across a recreation ground into Washford. This is not an old village. Once it was merely Watchetford, the ford on the way to Watchet. When the nearby Cistercian Abbey was founded in the thirteenth century it took its name from the established village of Cleeve, now known as Old Cleeve, a mile away to the north. The walk proceeds by lane and path to Washford Station. Along the way the view through the railway bridge on the right reveals some stone steps heading up a bank. Extensive excavations were made when the railway was constructed and it is thought that these were built to replace earlier steps which had been used by pilgrims walking from Cleeve Abbey to the former pilgrimage chapel on the coast.

The founding of Cistercian abbeys depended on the generosity of feudal Norman lords, but the monks always sought quiet places surrounded by good fertile land. Cleeve Abbey was founded by the Earl of Roumare whose family came from Roumare near Rouen in Normandy. His grandfather had earlier founded Revesby Abbey in Lincolnshire, then a lonely place in thick woodland on the edge of the undrained Fens, and it was from here that the first abbot and monks came to found Cleeve Abbey. Its official name, Vallis Florida, fitted the lush peaceful setting but never gained general acceptance.

The abbey had its ups and downs over the centuries which followed but survived until dissolution in 1537 when the abbot was pensioned off and the monks received gratuities. The extensive good farmland owned by the abbey would have provided the Crown with some rich pickings at this time. Most of the abbey's utilitarian buildings have survived because they were capable of being put to farming and domestic uses. There was no such alternative for the church and it appears to have been demolished shortly after dissolution. No doubt the dressed stones would have provided convenient building material for new homes and buildings in the locality. I find it difficult to reconcile our knowledge of the religious and superstitious beliefs of that time with the apparently uncaring way with which this desecration was carried out. However it is only one of many similar examples across the country.

The route turns left at the A39 and then right along a footpath at the side of a filling station. This leads to open countryside. Cleeve Abbey can be reached by continuing along the main road and then turning right. Nothing resembling these buildings will be seen again in the harsh upland country which lies ahead. A few steps from the busy main road lead to peace as the path rises gently along field edges. Maps show this path as part of a continuing line of lane and tracks which climbs up and then crosses the high country ahead. While proceeding in the same general direction, this line always ascends and never passes through a settlement of any consequence, features which are often hallmarks of ancient routes used by pack animals and burdened humans to avoid all unnecessary ups and downs. This one probably connected the old port of Watchet with outlying upland areas. From near the start, the highest point of the way is marked by distant conifers on the skyline to the right of front and these will be reached on a gentle curving ascent.

At first most of the surrounding farmland is arable. I recently came this way on a hot high summer day and was astonished to encounter a field of harvested wheat neatly set out in stocks. This all but forgotten scene immediately took me back to my boyhood days, a time when the small family farms on the heavy clay land of my home village still employed horse drawn sail reapers and casual workers for harvesting. Sheave making and stook building were hot, sticky and dusty work.

Tractors only began to make an appearance during the war years and combine harvesters came much later. I have since discovered that this field was harvested in the traditional manner to preserve the straw for repairs to the many surviving thatch roofs of the region.

This link with the past reminded me of other radical agricultural changes during my lifetime. Nowadays the outstanding feature of arable England is its emptiness and loneliness, a fact which struck me most forcibly as I made my way on foot across the Midlands some years ago. The complete mechanisation of arable farming during the last fifty years has led to a dramatic decline in the number of farm workers. Once numerous labourers would have rested on their tools and exchanged greetings with passing foot travellers but now, on the rare occasions that they are visible, it is as remote individuals incarcerated in tractor cabs, often enveloped in the sound of radios and completely divorced from the real world.

Today there are several seasons, particularly at the dead of winter and in between tending the growing crops and waiting for them to come to fruition, when the arable countryside of England is more empty of people than it has ever been since the Black Death and probably long before. I find this a haunting emptiness, far more uncanny than that of wild moors and mountains because everywhere remains well tended. It is a riddle of our time that while we live in a very crowded country, our countryside is now all but deserted.

Although there is nothing to show it, one mile from the filling station and at the spot where the path becomes a country lane for short distance, the route joins the boundary of Exmoor National Park. Two thirds of a mile further on, the Park is entered and the walk will remain within its bounds until the final approach to Minehead. I do not know who the felon of Felon's Oak might have been nor if he came to a sticky end here but nowadays there are several oaks at the spot. From here the route steepens and becomes a sunken hedge-bordered track with no distant views.

On an earlier winter occasion increasing height was proclaimed by the growing chill of the air as the grass underfoot, initially soaking wet, gradually became encrusted with moist snow and then by dry white powder. For the first time virgin rock appears along the way. Finally the track enters the very large rough and exposed pasture at Monkslade Common which serves as a home for both cattle and sheep. This hillside faces east and is a bitterly cold spot when winter winds blow from that quarter. By now all traces of arable land have gone. The next occasion will be on crossing the Vale of Porlock during the final stage of the walk.

From here there is a gentle climb to the broad hilltop through the conifer woods of Monkham Hill, first seen from faraway Washford. Compensation for the recent climb comes in the form of a well made near-level forest track which encourages a fast steady walking pace. Even up here a summer's day can be calm and hot, completely belying the severe weather experienced at other times. However these special days in this conifer forest also draw attention to its pervasive lifelessness. The dark needle-covered sterile ground beneath the thick tree cover contrasts sharply with the bright sun above and few sounds of birds and insects hang in the air.

The names Monkslade Common and Monkham Hill probably refer to the monks of Cleeve Abbey who had an outlying grange at nearby Luxborough. Beyond the shallow rise of Monkham Hill, which at around 1250 feet is the high point of this stage, the track slopes down to a meeting of ways above Perley Combe.

Here the combination of path, lane and tracks followed for 5 miles from Washford and which heads on to Timberscombe and beyond is exchanged for another track leading north and downhill in the direction of Dunster.

The scene now changes. On the right the lovely heather-covered moorland top of Withycombe Common gradually descends to Black Hill and on the left massed conifers eventually give way to native broadleaves with birch and sessile oak predominating. On sunny summer days this new environment contrasts sharply with the one immediately above, for here the warm air is full of the sights and sounds of birds and insects. Further down the woodland has the delightful name of Withycombe Scruffets. For centuries coppicing of the native oak, birch and ash provided fuel, building materials, fencing and tannin for the inhabitants of the farmland below. These woods remain in their original state and today provide great pleasure for all who pass by.

On reaching a track junction further down, the route turns left, heading into Long Combe. Although this resembles other Exmoor valleys, for reasons which have never been clear, it is a special favourite of mine. Perhaps the great solitude of the place casts a unique spell or maybe the surroundings remind me of past pleasures in similar circumstances. The path curves round and down the valley side through ancient stunted oaks clinging to the steep slope before meeting the stream in the bottom. Above, ranks of conifers stand stiffly to attention. This bottom is narrow with both path and stream continually vying for space and the water repeatedly crosses the way. In summer months jumping across these clear fords provides a pleasant pastime but the discoloured torrents of winter can present a barrier.

The valley eventually widens with rough meadows appearing on the left and other tracks join from both sides. At a place where the valley swings away to the left the route climbs up the hill ahead to the north.

During the course of the climb trees fall away to be replaced by brambles, bushes, heather and grass. Then a sinuous bank comes into view ahead. At one time it was thought to be a relic of the Civil War sieges of Dunster Castle which at different times was held by the opposing sides. However more recent thinking associates the bank with the much older circular earthwork known as Bat's Castle. This is a circular fort crowning the top of the hill and dates from Iron Age times. It can be regarded as a predecessor of the old fortified town of Dunster immediately below. Although only some 600 feet above sea level, Bat's Castle is open to the north and the sea and can be a very exposed in winter and is not a spot where folk would willingly choose to live for an extended period. However these fortifications, part of a pattern spread across the length and breadth of the land, reflect the dire needs of a time when the climate was deteriorating and pressures on farmland were growing due to the arrival of Celtic invaders from the Continent.

The views from the Castle are extensive, encompassing the sea, where nearby Steep Holm occupies centre stage, and a wide panorama of hills. The latter includes steep Grabbist Hill across the valley ahead and further away the rounded slopes of Dunkery Beacon, Exmoor's highest hill. Both will be climbed at a later stage. Nearby Gallox Hill is reached across a small dip. It too has a circular earthwork on its summit and is thought to be contemporary with Bat's Castle. 'Gallox' may sound pleasant but it has a very grim connotation, being a corruption of 'Gallows'. The gallows in question are not thought to have been up here but next to Gallox Bridge at the entry to Dunster.

Beyond the top of Gallox Hill the path descends to trees before turning right and down to join a well-used wooded track leading to Gallox Bridge. This is old, narrow, double-arched and built of stone. In medieval times it stood at the head of an inlet of the sea or marshy ground, now transformed to level green meadows. Consequently all roads from the town to the south and east once came this way.

The present secluded meeting place of wooded tracks on the approach to the bridge would then have been a busy crossroads. It was here that the gallows are believed to have been placed to remind local inhabitants of the ultimate penalty for a whole host of wrong doings, many of which would now be regarded as minor offences.

In 1685 three local men, Monmouth rebels who had been captured at the battle of Sedgemoor, were executed here in a gruesome manner as part of a pattern of severe retribution exacted across the West Country. The Crown's aim was to stifle any further opposition to King James II's regime. Ironically he soon departed in haste without a fight. Unfortunately the effect of this punishment on the population at large appears to have been much more enduring. It has been said that the trauma caused by these brutal acts was so deep and has remained so long in public consciousness that the West has never since

Bat's Castle

played any major role in the political life of the nation.

The central pier between the two arches of Gallox Bridge is buttressed to cleave the onslaughts of brown water which periodically pour down from the nearby hills. Beyond the water the crowded buildings of Dunster begin where they have done for centuries.

Dunster, one of the best preserved medieval towns in the country, is enhanced by its picturesque setting in a narrow valley leading out through sea marshes to the Bristol Channel. A commanding tor overlooks the site of the town and lovely high wooded hills stand on the other three sides. The centre piece of the whole is the restored castle, a castellated house, which stands close to the steep tor which was once surmounted by the old Norman keep. Below, sheltered by the surrounding higher ground, the buildings of the little town crowd into a shallow basin. Many have medieval features, including the priory, the priory church, the tithe barn, the water mill, the Nuns House, the much photographed Yarn Market and even an old dovecot. The wool and weaving trade which once brought prosperity has long since gone and consequently the town has never grown beyond its medieval bounds. Its layout also remains unchanged, from the buildings squeezed together along the main streets to the long thin burgage strips stretched out behind them.

Dunster and its lovely surroundings inspired Cecil Frances Alexander to compose the lines of her popular hymn 'All things bright and beautiful'. Her words about the flowers, birds, fruits, meadows, trees, the river, the summer sun and winter wind all ring true but not, perhaps, her description of Grabbist Hill as a 'purple headed mountain'. Nowadays her verse about the rich man in his castle and the poor man at his gate, each in his proper place, is often omitted.

My feelings for Dunster are of affection tempered with reservation. The little town went into decline long ago and the long peace and quiet which followed has made it vulnerable to pressures created by the modern tourist industry. During winter the town may appear much as it once did but in summer months visitors crowd the streets, hovering around the many tea and gift shops where in former times local craftsmen employed their skills and services to meet the needs of their community. The overall effect of today's pressures is twofold. In season the intense activity completely masks the attractive old inanimate features of the place and sadly out of it there is a pervasive impression of a town which has lost its heart. Dunster is only 2 miles from Minehead and there is a regular bus service between the two.

Gallox Bridge

⇥ STAGE 3 ⇤

DUNSTER TO HORNER

From Dunster the walk continues along the ridge to the west, heading for Wootton Courtenay. From there the edge of the upper Vale of Porlock is followed to Horner. This stage is relatively short, so before setting out there will be time to wander around Dunster and its castle and perhaps spot the Civil War cannon-ball hole in the rafters of the Yarn Market.

Dunster Castle's appearance dates back to the Civil War. When that conflict ended the defences were slighted to discourage any further rebellious use. The original keep which stood on top of today's tall wooded knoll was destroyed and so were the curtain walls. However the original gatehouse and the house which had been built at a later date in the castle outer ward were both spared. The latter was subsequently modified and its mock medieval decorations now contribute much to the romantic appeal of the surroundings.

This stage commences with a climb up Grabbist Hill, a steep rise marking the beginning of a prominent ridge which extends westwards for 3 miles. The northern slopes are gentle, broken by attractive winding combes, but those on the south are impressive, standing high above the Avill Valley. Trees are almost everywhere in the form of forestry plantations, except for one part of the top which is open moorland. The route starts from the market place, following Priory Green round the back of old burgage strips behind the High Street and then passes through the former priory to the primary school. From here a tarmac track heads uphill past an old cemetery and allotments to a gate below the wooded hillside. A right turn is followed by a climb through trees to a left one onto a track heading to the top of the hill. There are other ways up Grabbist Hill but this is the easiest.

The crowded buildings of Dunster soon disappear behind trees and at the top rough meadows often provide grazing for a herd of red deer. The sight of these creatures against a backdrop of Minehead's many roofs with the open sea beyond makes a most unusual picture. The track, heading west, then leaves the trees and bushes behind to emerge onto the moorland area of the ridge. In late summer this is one of nature's beautiful gardens, full of the brilliant yellows and purples of gorse and heather. On the left a deep trough marks the Avill Valley and beyond the ground rises to the forested heights of Croydon Hill. The sea lies on the right and to the rear the distant Quantocks roll inland away from the coast. This broad open ridge may seem an innocuous place but I have not always found it so. The elements have a major impact on all walks and when I first came upon the present scene in 1951, this truism was about to be confirmed with a vengeance.

It was a blustery, sunny and showery September day and by late morning my old school friend and I were heading away from Dunster up the sheltered side of the hill. On reaching the top and leaving the trees behind, to our amazement we met a horrendous gale which immediately tipped both of us off our feet. This was a challenge which the young were not prepared to yield without a fight. In the breathtaking struggle which followed, progress came in a series of oblique crab-like advances between the worst forays. For a long time the shelter of the trees ahead seemed an impossible goal but finally, and by now exhausted, we crawled on all fours into the lee of their earthen boundary bank. That event was almost fifty years ago, my companion of the day has long since departed this earth and my memories of many succeeding events have faded away, but this one never will.

The track along the hilltop was probably another old highway linking Dunster with outlying areas. After passing a young plantation it reaches mature trees, possibly the ones which provided the much needed shelter long ago. Soon trees are on all sides and the way ahead is a broad gently undulating track through a succession of very quiet places. Although the edge of Minehead is only a mile away, few people come up here. On each side native beech, birch and oak screen the rows of conifers beyond. This is one of many wonderful local places which can restore peace of mind to those who have spent too long in traffic and towns.

Near the concrete Ordnance Survey point marking the spot height of two hundred and ninety five metres, the route leaves the ridge for another track on the left which leads down to Wootton Courtenay. This soon reduces to a path and then drops steeply through old heavily wooded enclosures. A stile appears ahead, revealing a descending meadow beyond. After the enclosing woodland, the new scene is a delight. In the foreground the saddleback tower of Wootton Courtenay's church stands above a small vineyard and beyond rounded heather slopes climb ever more gently to the tops of Robin How and Janey How, twin high points at the eastern end of the Dunkery range, their summits crowned by Bronze Age burial mounds.

From the bottom of the meadow the route heads right onto the lane through the village, passing the church and the village shop before turning onto the dead-end lane which leads to Brockwell. Beyond the last dwelling at the road end the walk does not take any of the uphill tracks and paths but instead follows a level track to the right heading north west along the hill foot.

Old quarries on the hillside above Brockwell were once a source of high grade iron ore which was transported along this track by pack horse and cart to Porlock Weir for shipment to the steel furnaces of South Wales. Nowadays the

Church and vinyard at Wootton Courtenay with the Dunkery ridge in the background

overgrown parts of the track would no longer permit the passage of horse drawn vehicles. The uneven ground surface of the old workings has also been reclaimed by vegetation, with the exception of an occasional exposed lump of red rock, very heavy and rich with iron. At this point the configuration of the surrounding high hills suggests that the upper part of the Avill Valley draining to Dunster, and the Vale of Porlock are one and the same but their subtle watershed is already behind, somewhere between Wootton Courtenay and Brockwell. Then as the walk proceeds, the true nature of the Vale becomes apparent, with the hilly fields on the right beginning to roll down towards the sea at Porlock bay. On the left a line of old enclosures extend to the beginning of the open moor above. Further along this reclaimed land becomes increasingly unkempt, until at Woodcock Gardens its old banks now encircle a nature reserve in the care of the Exmoor Natural History Society.

The story of this particular enclosure provides an insight to the history of the region. At the end of the Napoleonic Wars farming went into decline and there were many hungry mouths in the locality. These enclosures were reclaimed by manual labour from the open moor at this time. One can only wonder at the amount of digging, enclosing, manuring and liming that would have been carried out by the first tenants to convert this acid open moor into satisfactory vegetable plots. Alas their efforts were only short lived. Over the years many local inhabitants moved away to the growing industrial towns or emigrated abroad. The last time that Woodcock Gardens are known to have been worked as intended was immediately after the First World War, another period of severe farming depression.

The gardens were purchased in the 1930s as a house site but the project fell through, probably due to access problems and lack of a suitable water supply. Since then slow reversion to moorland has taken place and the process was already well advanced when the Exmoor Natural History Society came on the scene. Their efforts are now aimed at maintaining the present status quo. A short diversion into the gardens is well worthwhile to observe the variety of flora and fauna which now thrive in this semi-wild place.

Another range of hills, topped by Selworthy Beacon, has now come into view to the north and will remain visible almost to Horner. Selworthy's white church, set on the hillside, is a continuing feature of this range, apparently pushing trees aside in order to peer out at the wider world. There are many corners of Exmoor where I would have liked this walk to have gone and Selworthy is one of them, not so much for the village itself but for the many paths, lovely wooded hillsides and the moorland top in the vicinity. However if I had succumbed to this temptation the walk would have become inordinately long and most erratic.

Selworthy is often considered to be the perfect example of an old world English village but reality is rather different. The group of lovely thatched cottages, arranged around the green below the church and towering trees, has never been a working village in its present form but a group of retirement homes built and renovated by the Acland family for their retired estate workers. The family benevolence continued into the twentieth century when they presented the whole of their Holnicote Estate to the nation. This extends all the way from the sea to the top of Dunkery Beacon. The present stage of the walk entered the estate after Brockwell and much of Stage Four to Dunkery and beyond and almost the whole of Stage Ten along the coast lie within its bounds. The estate is an Exmoor in miniature, containing examples of almost every type of local scene. These range from a high wild coast to heather moorland with deep wooded valleys, farmland and attractive old villages in between. The National Trust now have the whole in their care.

The present track now follows a boundary between land reclaimed for farming long ago and that which has remained in a wild or semi-wild state. Thus the route traces a frontier of civilisation. Glimpses of the rolling neatly hedged meadows and old farms below on the right contrast sharply with the empty moor above on the left. Later the trees on the hillside become dense, obstructing all further views of the high moor. The present track can be followed to Horner but there is a worthwhile short detour to the village of Luccombe. The name 'Luccombe' is said to mean 'enclosed valley' and it is appropriate. Dunkery's high moorland looms to the south and nearby hillocks of small hedged meadows crowd in on the other three sides, making the village all but invisible from all points of the compass.

The track leaves the woods through a gate beside two old cottages and enters Stoney Street which nowadays belies its name with a covering of smooth tarmac. The way passes old cottages enhanced by many flowers in summer months. At the centre there is a part-time shop, a village hall not much larger than a sitting room and an attractive church with a lofty tower. The last contains a special feature. On the floor of the nave in front of the choir there is a small mat.

When this is moved aside the memorial plate to William Harrison inscribed with his full length portrait comes into view. He was a village elder who died at the age of seventy six in 1615. The ruff around his neck immediately captures the eye because it is of phenomenal size and appears most uncomfortable.

Outside in the churchyard there is the broken stump of a cross said to have been decapitated during Oliver Cromwell's time. Damage to many church buildings in England is often wrongly blamed on Cromwell's men, to the extent that the phrase 'one of the ruins which Cromwell knocked about a bit' became the theme of a music hall song and has passed into the language. No doubt these soldiers did do some damage but it was by no means all that they are now blamed for. By the time of the Civil War, the reformation of the church, starting with the Dissolution of Monasteries, had been under way for a century. So had the wholesale removal and destruction of what were considered to be graven images from churches and cathedrals. After the Civil War and restoration of the monarchy, there was widespread revulsion for this past church damage and in seeking someone to blame the then out of favour Parliamentarians proved convenient scapegoats. In reality responsibility for most of this despoliation had lain much closer to home with the church authorities themselves. Unfortunately this falsehood has been allowed to masquerade as truth ever since.

The walk continues past the church tower, out of the churchyard and onto a path where it turns right. In summertime this is a way of dreams. Most Exmoor tracks and paths are stony and sometimes muddy but this one is unique with a well mown cushioned surface very kind to the feet. In addition the carefully

Stoney Street, Luccombe

trimmed hedges on each side match this excellence and never ensnare a walker's clothing.

The path ends at the lane from Luccombe to Horner and this is followed for approximately 300 yards to the road junction known as Chapel Cross.

Beyond this a wide verge on the right reveals the foundations of a former stone building. These are the paltry remains of a humble wayside chapel which long ago was abused in the same manner as Cleeve Abbey Church, the missing masonry probably being re-used locally. Nearby Chapel Cross and the adjacent Chapel Steep are well known but nowadays few speeding travellers will appreciate the reason for their names.

The route goes through the gate opposite and rejoins the track through trees which follows the farmland boundary. This leads to Horner half a mile away. With continuing progress the distant view to the north has opened out. The steep wooded hillside around Selworthy has now been exchanged for the grass and heather-covered rounded top of Bossington Hill next to an enticing glimpse of open sea. This corner of Exmoor is a particular favourite of mine and will be traversed during the final stage of the walk.

The track ahead suddenly veers to the right, is joined by others and then enters the lane close to Horner. This small hamlet of stone houses with tiled roofs has two tea gardens open in season, a carpark, public toilets and an old water mill now converted into a home.

The Broken Cross at Luccombe

⇢ STAGE 4 ⇥

HORNER TO EXFORD

The walk now climbs over Dunkery Beacon before descending to Exford. The scenery is magnificent and the distance moderate but the route is exposed for 3 miles over the highest ground.

The hamlet of Horner takes its name from nearby Horner Water which drains both the north side of the Dunkery range and the high ground further to the west. It is said to derive from the Celtic word 'hwrnwr', meaning 'snorer'. Having listened to the river from near and far in all weathers, seasons and conditions of flow, I have to say that I have never heard anything remotely like the sound of snoring. There is another naming oddity: the river does not have one but three. Near its source close to Alderman's Barrow it is known as Chetsford Water, further down as Nutscale Water and finally only becomes Horner Water in the vicinity of Pool Bridge 2½ miles above Horner. One could speculate that Exmoor folk in the old days did not travel far from home.

This stage passes over Dunkery Beacon, at 1705 feet the highest place on Exmoor. It fills its lordly role well, with impressive rounded tops facing north and a majestic cloak of brilliant purple heather in high summer. From Horner the high ground is reached along two beautiful wild wooded valleys. Starting behind the converted Horner Mill, the path heads upstream along the mill leat into Horner Valley. This is a delectable alternative to the more popular track up the valley on the opposite side of Horner Water.

As the path heads away the buildings quickly disappear from view, soon followed by the narrow meadows beside the river. Now trees are everywhere, overhanging the rapid rock-strewn water on the valley floor and climbing away out of sight up the steep hillsides. These are the native trees of the country, a mix of oak, beech, birch and an occasional holly. Finally beyond the entrance to the leat the scene is reduced to just three components, sky, trees and river.

These idyllic sylvan surroundings seem unchanged for thousands of years but this is not so. For some time it had been known that coppicing and charcoal burning had been carried out here and recently evidence has come to light of an Iron Age fort, the remains of a fourteenth century agricultural settlement and a major post-medieval iron smelting and forging works. These are typical examples of the flow and ebb of civilisation across Exmoor.

The path approaches a footbridge over Horner Water which gives access to the main track up the valley. The present path is satisfactory for much of the way but if the river is in spate a small section may be flooded. If so it is advisable to cross the bridge here and follow the main track up to East Water.

The continuing path now becomes more challenging, being rough, hilly and sometimes passing high above the water. But it is also most pleasurable. As the river winds its way back into the hills height is continually being gained.

Due to dense summer foliage and the need to concentrate on the ground underfoot, the confluence of Horner Water and East Water is easily overlooked. The only obvious sign is the majestic creeper-hung oaks which grow in this well-watered sheltered place. However confirmation eventually comes when the path returns to the stream edge and the diminished flow of East Water becomes obvious.

The path joins the bridleway beside East Water, following it for almost a mile. The water continually crosses and recrosses the track along the now confined valley bottom. Fortunately there are wooden footbridges beside each ford.

Earlier the water had scurried and splashed along its stone-strewn bed but now it hurtles over boulders, at one spot pouring over a small waterfall. Further change comes with a lane heading down the opposite hillside to cross the stream at a ford. Here the walk turns left over the footbridge beside the ford and the road is followed for a short distance before turning right into steep, tall Hollow Combe.

The climb which began gently back at Horner has now become distinctly steep. The surrounding trees have thinned out and an occasional rowan has made an appearance. Although the nearby oaks have grown to a majestic size in this high but sheltered place, there is a pervasive sense of change to come. The path crosses a tiny stream in the bottom of the steep combe. Here the watershed of the Dunkery ridge is only half a mile away. Yet two miles in the opposite direction at Horner the flow has become a sizable river, proof that Exmoor's small trickles soon grow into large torrents.

Beyond the combe bottom the path climbs a few steps to a junction. As height has consistently been gained, there is a tendency to follow the

East Water

ascending branch on the left rather than the other which descends. However after a short climb the left branch turns downhill and the correct right one soon regains its lost height and continues upwards.

The surrounding trees are now smaller and, with one of those sudden changes characteristic of Exmoor, the path emerges onto the open hillside. Only small lonely rowans and a few thorn bushes survive in the midst of the bracken up here.

There are now extensive views to the north. Immediately below, the well wooded winding trough of East Water leads down to the Horner Valley which in turn weaves its way through and out of the hills into the Vale of Porlock. The dominant feature of this scene is Bossington Hill, standing proud above the Vale of Porlock, and beyond it the sea stretches away to distant Wales. This wide panorama contains a feature, which although small, soon catches the eye, the facing wing of Cloutsham Farm. This, the last surviving settlement in the vicinity, stands among its meadows on a promontory of high ground between the wild woods of the East Water and Horner Water valleys. The eye-catching detail is in the form of a Swiss chalet, an unexpected feature in this spacious Exmoor scene. It was built by the Aclands at a time in the nineteenth century when Swiss architecture was popular and the family are said to have used it for entertainment purposes during their annual holidays at Holnicote House.

At a junction on the open hillside the route turns left and uphill to Dicky's Path, named after Sir Richard Acland, and then turns right. This new path climbs gently across the face of the hill below Dunkery's summit before descending into the wooded nook marking the upper reaches of Aller Combe. This spot is the only place of shelter for a considerable distance and, if needed, can provide protection from both wind and rain.

On leaving the diminutive stream and its trees behind, the path climbs towards the remains of the Iron Age settlement at Sweetworthy. Some of the earthworks are on the open moor and others in the reclaimed meadow below the line of mature beeches. Little is known about this settlement which is not in a naturally defensive position and may have been occupied long after the Iron Age. As traces of medieval Bagley also lie in the combe below, these provide clear evidence that numbers of people lived up here for a very long time. Now only Cloutsham remains.

Red deer often graze and rest in the meadows below the beeches and at first sight can be mistaken for farm animals. Here the route leaves Dicky's Path and heads straight up a well beaten track to the summit of Dunkery. During the climb bracken is replaced by a carpet of heather, the crowning glory of the ridge in late summer.

The final steep slope ends abruptly and the summit of Dunkery Beacon comes into view. There is a large cairn commemorating the donation of the hill to the

Dunkery Beacon

nation, a direction indicator and several nondescript piles of stones. Erosion caused by many visiting hooves and feet is also evident. The hill takes its name from a combination of the Old English 'dun' meaning 'hill' and the Celtic 'creag' which implies a rocky place and is related to the modern word 'crag'.

This hilltop would not normally be considered rocky but it does have more stones on display than many Exmoor hills. The second word 'Beacon' comes from its use as a warning fire beacon over hundreds of years. Although often cold, windy and bleak, the Beacon is nowadays noted for the presence of people, many of whom arrive on foot from cars parked beside the road half a mile away to the east. The frequent proximity of minor modern roads to the tops of Exmoor hills dates back to the time when they served as important trade routes.

Only once have I enjoyed Dunkery Beacon all to myself and that was a very special occasion. It took place towards the end of a cross-England walk. Due to delay I did not arrive here until a late October day. The weather when I set out from Wootton Courtenay was foul, dark with driving rain. Plodding up the path to the summit, which by then had become a running stream, I was apprehensive about the hours ahead. Suddenly and unexpectedly the rain ceased. Then a small patch of blue appeared in the sky, just big enough to make a very small sailor a pair of trousers. At the very moment I reached the top the sun came out. In this new crystal-clear light each soaking wet stone and pebble on the summit sparkled more brightly than large diamonds can ever do. But the span of time was very brief because, as the water began to drain away, the sparkle faded. However for that magical fleeting moment I had enjoyed a very special Dunkery all to myself and it had been a great privilege.

The wide view from the top embraces nearby moorland, prominent hills along the coast, a hint of the Vale of Porlock and also a dramatic change. The Bristol Channel now appears so narrow that it has allowed the coast, hills and mountains of Wales to creep very close. Conversely towards the south the hills fall slowly to the distant farmland of mid Devon and beyond this a long dark mass against the sky marks the hills and tors of Dartmoor.

Restless humanity is left behind a few steps to the west of the summit and replaced by the peace of the moor. The walk now heads westwards for a mile along a distinct but rather roughly formed path leading to Rowbarrows. This final rise at the western end of the Dunkery range is named after several Bronze Age burial mounds scattered around its top. As the summit is nearly flat, only one tomb known as Little Rowbarrow, projecting above a false skyline, is obvious from the east. In full view from Dunkery Beacon and all intermediate points this positioning would have been deliberate but the reason for it is unknown.

Nowadays it is difficult to picture the ancient scene when looking at the present one. In the kinder climate of the time, much of the present moorland top would have been covered with native forest and there might well have been processional ways through the trees. It is a sobering thought that although the descendants of these ancient peoples are still with us, it is unlikely that we will ever have a clear understanding of their ancestors' religious beliefs and practices.

From Rowbarrows the route begins to head away from the moorland top. The initial objective is a straggling overgrown beech hedge a quarter of a mile to the south. This borders high rough meadows where the ground drops away more steeply. There is no direct footpath from Rowbarrows to the hedge and a detour is necessary to avoid crossing the heather. This follows a path, initially rather obscure, which heads south-east before joining an obvious track along the uphill side of the beech hedge. Here the route turns west.

The moorland on the more familiar north side of Dunkery extends downhill for a considerable distance, so the presence of enclosures high on its southern slopes may come as a surprise. The top hedge of these pastures, now on the immediate left, reaches a height of 1560 feet, nearly that of Dunkery Beacon itself. The explanation for the marked difference between the two sides of the hill could lie in different land ownership and management patterns in the past but a more cogent reason might be the relative warmth of these south facing hillsides and their more gentle gradients. Although the top enclosures nowadays appear neglected they still provide pasture for cattle and sheep during the summer months.

The track beside the beech hedge continues westwards for a mile before entering a lane at a road junction. The walk then follows this lane to the south

Dunkery Beacon

west for further half mile. Lovely heather moorland still stretches away on the right but the beech hedge on the left has now become thick and well tended. At the next road junction the route turns left along a track enclosed by tall beech hedges.

Once again sudden transition from miles of open space to intimate surroundings delivers a sharp shock to the senses.

Ahead the route turns right through a field gate into meadows and the descent to Exford begins in earnest. These verdant lower meadows with their kinder climate provide a home for many sheep. At length the way becomes a hedge enclosed track with the old cobbling patched by concrete and tarmac. As the descent continues the first tall trees are passed by since leaving Hollow Combe, now many miles to the rear. Finally, at the first isolated dwelling, the way becomes a tarmac lane and the village is not far away.

Exford will not surprise newcomers arriving from the present direction but those who first come by road might have expected a raw treeless upland settlement. Even the lowest point of the settlement, beside the river, is 820 feet above sea level. However the reality is a pleasant village in a valley sheltered by low hills covered in rich meadows, hedges and trees.

Exford, as it name suggests, developed beside the road at a ford over the River Exe. Now 6 miles from its source at Exe Head, a site which will be visited later, the river is already substantial and the present surroundings are very different from the bleak bare moorland of its birth. The small village clusters beside the river and along two sides of a recreation ground. Although ancient its present appearance does not give any impression of venerability because the old stone and thatch buildings associated with traditional farming were swept away in the nineteenth century to make way for Exmoor's first tourist wave which was based on hunting, shooting and fishing.

The church stands beside the road higher up the hill. This highway is an ancient route across Exmoor from Bridgwater to Barnstaple and was formerly known as the Harepath, an Anglo-Saxon name derived from the Heeren or Mens' Path, implying a route used by armies. However by the time these Germanic invaders arrived it had already been in use for several thousand years. The present church is believed to be the fourth on the site and the tower, the oldest part, only dates from the fifteenth century. The foundations of the original structure, a wayside chapel, may lie beneath the present building and this was dedicated to St Salvyn, another of those Celtic missionaries who arrived here from Wales during the Dark Ages.

Today's building is dedicated to Mary Magdalene. Exford is only small but has shops, accommodation, pubs and eating places. During summer months the 'North Exmoor Tourist Bus' passes through to Minehead.

⇥ STAGE 5 ⇤

EXFORD TO WITHYPOOL

The highest and most exposed parts of Exmoor are now behind. However this stage is challenging due to a combination of length and the number of hills along the way.

The watershed of the high moors was crossed at Dunkery Beacon and, by now several miles to the south, the two largest south flowing rivers of Exmoor, the Barle and the Exe, have grown to an appreciable size. Sections of their beautiful valleys lie ahead, separated by high farmland and moors. This stage passes through many different scenes but unlike the previous one where signs of man's efforts were sometimes scanty here they are always obvious. This part of the walk includes the southernmost point at Tarr Steps.

Exford is usually quiet but can become bedlam when several tourist coaches arrive simultaneously and disgorge their passengers at the small village centre.

However pulsating the centre might be, total peace reigns a few steps away. This stage starts at the entrance to the village car park which is littered with miscellaneous pieces of modern farm equipment, presumably awaiting repair.

Perhaps this untidiness should be forgiven because it represents the one remaining village craft out of many. Most small communities once had a number and these often included a blacksmith, cobbler, tailor, plumber, baker, chimney sweep and a joiner. Now modern roads and speedy transport have swept them all away.

The River Exe lies beyond the car park. Here on warm sunny days fish swim lazily against the steady flow, patiently waiting for food to come their way. At first the river wends its way through hedge-enclosed meadows in a broad valley, a scene which soon changes. The way leaves the river to follow a path signposted to Winsford and after crossing higher ground rejoins the water on the approach to Lyncombe. Hills are now rising on each side of the river. At Lyncombe, an attractive old house with disused farm buildings, the path becomes a bridleway.

The valley sides have now closed in, their wild sides, covered in bushes and bracken, are topped by overgrown beech hedges which stand out in lines against the sky like advancing armies of old. The track passes along the lovely valley side above the water. Further along towards Nethercote the steep slopes are covered with woodland and sheep meadows. On arriving at this old settlement, where in the past dogs might have been expected to bark on approach, there is now no sound. Here too the farm buildings appear unused.

Beyond the farm the River Exe is crossed by a bridge. Before finally leaving the stream opportunity should be taken to enjoy the sight and sound of its clear running waters. For most of the time they sing a very gentle song sliding along their stony bed past grassy banks and occasional large boulders. The next encounter with the river will be in very bleak surroundings. The present beautiful part of Exe Valley, flowing on down to Winsford, is gradually left behind on a long steady climb up the bridleway to Bye Common. The River Barle is the next objective but the Winn Brook lies between, so another climb and two descents lie immediately ahead.

To the rear Nethercote peeps out through trees in the valley bottom as in front the view gradually extends beyond the lush and wild Exe Valley walls. At the top of the long slope, the surrounding countryside comes into view for the first time, an extensive undulating green plateau of hedge-bordered meadows sundered by the lovely sinuous trough of the Exe winding its way through their midst. This surrounding high farm country may be pleasant to the eye but has no special appeal for me.

On entering the meadows at the top of the hill the way forward is not clear but a standing stone and nearby signpost at the junction of two almost invisible bridleways in the middle of a field provide waymarks. From here the way can be determined from the O.S. map which shows the line of the obscure route in relation to the visible field boundaries. At length the walk emerges onto the often busy Winsford-Withypool road and turns right.

Country highways which lack footpaths or even secure verges and are used by speeding traffic are an anathema to walkers. The Winsford-Withypool road often falls in this category. However after a third of a mile escape comes in the form of a track through meadows to Withycombe Farm beside the Winn Brook. Along the way the new peaceful scene opens out to reveal striking distant features. To the front the steep bank of Burrow Wood rises from the valley floor and on its right a deep gouge in the hillside marks The Punchbowl with the curving moorland top of Winsford Hill above.

The Punchbowl is something of an Exmoor curiosity. There are many steep hillsides in the region but those inland are usually associated with substantial streams. Here only a trickle emerges from the bottom of the large deep basin set into the side of the hill. As the feature faces north I have wondered whether it might have been the site of a slush glacier. Although the vicinity was not covered with thick ice during the Ice Ages, the climate would have been very cold for a very long time.

After passing the farm buildings, a track, initially rather obscure, climbs through a meadow before mounting the western rim of The Punchbowl. During the ascent the track changes to a close eroded strip of grass through heather. A short detour can be made to the top of Winsford Hill and its attendant Bronze Age burial mounds known as Wambarrows which show signs of past rifling. The next objective stands near Spire Cross three quarters of a mile to the southeast. It can be reached by one of several paths across the moor or by following the strip of close-cropped grass beside the road heading in the same direction.

In spite of its name. Spire Cross has no connection with a church. The 'Cross' refers to the nearby cross roads and the 'Spire' to an old local word for rushes. Presumably the latter grew at Spire, a small settlement in the combe immediately below. Spire is at the head of the Little River, one of the smaller Barle tributaries which enters the main stream near Tarr Steps.

Although Christian connections are lacking, this spot definitely has some historic ones. These are associated with a small structure 200 yards to the east of the crossroads. At a distance it appears to consist of four stone pillars

The Caratacus Stone and its distinctive shelter

supporting a pitched roof but on approach a leaning stone can be seen within. The structure is relatively modern and the stone very old. On one of its faces there is a crude inscription in Roman lettering of the type used in the fifth and sixth centuries which has been deciphered as 'kinsman of Caratacus'.

It is not known whether this Caratacus was the famous king of the Silures in South Wales who opposed the Roman invasion or, as is more likely, someone who was named after him. It has also been postulated that the stone is a prehistoric monument and stood on this site long before the inscription was cut. Several ancient trackways and the Bronze Age memorials on Winsford Hill are all close by.

Standing stones attract legends of two broad but very different types. One is that they bring bad luck to those who move them and the other that they mark the site of buried treasure and therefore invite disturbance. More often than not greed has overcome superstition and as recently as the inter-war years the Caratacus Stone was thrown down by unknown individuals who were presumably seeking riches. My guess is that this was only the last of many similar incidents throughout its long history.

From Spire Cross the way is along the lane heading south-west. At the point where the road leaves the moor there is a track on the right which continues along the moorland edge. After a third of a mile this bridleway turns abruptly into a hedge bordered track through fields. At one moment open moorland stretches away on the right and at the next there is only intimate enclosure in the midst of agricultural land. The way is now downhill to the old settlement of Knaplock and after passing these buildings it follows Watery Lane. The descent from the edge of the moor continues. Bushes beside the track give way to native trees and, as befits its name, the sound of running water grows on the left. The trees become taller and then, suddenly, the bottom of the Barle valley and its broad river come into view. The way is now to the left along a well used track following the water downstream.

The Barle is a much more impressive river than the Exe left behind at Nethercote. Like its partner, it constantly twists and turns through the surrounding high country, with the water alternately rushing over masses of rock and then tarrying for a short while in quiet pools. Tall trees overhang the river and on fine summer days many tiny patches of sunlight penetrate through the thick foliage to create a host of fleeting dancing stars on its moving surface. Here, water, rocks and trees are the constantly changing components of a succession of intimate scenes. Rapid scene changes and a lack of distant views make map reading difficult but there is no need for this because the well blazed path continues steadily onwards beside the water.

I have often wondered why the more impressive Barle has given precedence to the Exe. Their sources are adjacent in the high country long known as the Forest of Exmoor and at their meeting below Dulverton the combined waters continue on as the Exe.

During warm summer holidays, the noise of the young can reach the ear long before Tarr Steps come into view. Then on arrival the extent of distraction from children playing, paddling, splashing, shouting and even proceeding on erratic voyages in inflatable dinghies is such that the new surroundings and even the bridge known as Tarr Steps fail to make any initial impression.

The water is broader here, shallow and relatively placid, bounded by a meadow on one side, trees on the other and crossed by Tarr Steps, an impressive clapper bridge. Back in the old packhorse days an important trade route came this way. Elsewhere on Exmoor there are old stone bridges for wheeled traffic, pack horse bridges and stepping stones but nothing quite like this and as a result it has long been a focus of attention.

At one time the bridge was thought to be prehistoric but recent thinking favours the medieval period, an age corresponding to that of its many counterparts on neighbouring Dartmoor. The typical placid mood of the river may seem permanent but at times the waters can become very angry indeed. One occasion coincided with the Lynmouth flood disaster in 1952 when the

A glimpse of Tarr Steps

Barle's flood waters dislodged all but two of the spans. Afterwards the large stones were replaced by members of the army using mechanical equipment.

Both interest and puzzlement have centred on the origin of Tarr Steps, probably because they are locally unusual and also because the adjacent broad shallow ford provided a satisfactory crossing under most conditions. In addition the construction of Tarr Steps would have required considerable effort at a time when local resources were limited. When earlier generations came across features in the landscape which were puzzling they were all too willing to believe that the supernatural had had a hand in them. Depending on the period the small people, fairies, the old Nordic gods and, of course, the Devil himself were considered responsible. It was so here. According to an old legend the Devil made the Steps when he had some spare time and after completing his work he liked to sunbathe on the stones.

Tarr Steps is the southern turning point of the walk. In addition to the bridge, on one side of the river there is a cafe-cum-shop, a carpark and toilets and on the other an hotel. The walk crosses the Steps and then heads upstream along the river's west bank. While proceeding over the stones in sunny weather, it might be a good idea to watch out for a recumbent figure with a tail and large pronged fork beside him.

Much as I like these surroundings they are not my favourite part of Exmoor, so with a thrill of pleasure my steps turn northwards, back towards the high empty hills and the mountainous coast. Although the path leading away from Tarr Steps is well used the sounds of voices and activity are soon left behind. Three quarters of a mile further upstream, beyond the initial point of entry to the east bank, the walk re-crosses the river by a footbridge. From here it continues northwards along a well trodden bridleway, in the opposite direction to the waters hurrying on down towards the distant south coast and the English Channel.

Further along, beyond the pronounced river meanders at steep sided Bradley and Pitt Woods, there is a marked change of scene. The high valley sides move away from the water, leaving the river meandering along a narrow flood plain clad in a mix of trees and meadows which has all the characteristics of classic beautiful parkland. The valley may still twist and turn as before and the river within these bounds even more so but now the flow is slower and there are only gentle ripples on its surface.

At South Hill, on the approach to Withypool, there are stepping stones across the river and the bridleway beyond provides a more direct approach to the village. Years ago, when walking around Exmoor in the opposite direction, my youngest son and I arrived here to find the stepping stones badly dislodged and the river running full. It was a cold Easter day but being unwilling to retrace our steps we crossed with boots removed and trousers rolled up. The experience was uncomfortable and somewhat hazardous. Since then the steps have been replaced but recently I noted that they are once again becoming skewed.

The most frequented way to Withypool follows the east bank of the river, along an undulating path with unpleasant muddy stretches after rain. The Withypool-Winsford road is joined a third of a mile to the east of the village.

Withypool is a pleasant place with well kept gardens, a post office, a shop and the Royal Oak Inn. Nowadays with good roads and transport it is part of the modern world but not long ago this was an isolated self-contained community in the middle of the moor, distanced by roads which were often near-impassable.

Even the local postman made his rounds on horseback. The village takes its name from the withies beside the river. The nearby handsome six-arched stone bridge is both the focal point and prime architectural feature of the settlement.

Withypool Bridge over the Barle

⤜ STAGE 6 ⤛

FROM WITHYPOOL TO SIMONSBATH

This short stage provides an easy day in the middle of the walk. Progress is made towards the high moors which divide southern Exmoor from the sea.

Although the River Barle passes through both Withypool and Simonsbath, the first 4 miles of this stage are not beside the river but along a low ridge to the north. There are excellent riverside paths both above and below this stretch but none here, an omission which is puzzling. The walk starts on the west side of the old Withypool village school, now an activity centre. From here a public footpath crosses four small meadows in turn. These are irregular in shape and enclosed by old beech hedges and mature trees, giving the impression of their piecemeal recovery from the moor a very long time ago. On reaching the highway known as Kitridge Lane, the route turns left.

At first the tall hedges on both sides of the highway permit only brief glimpses of heather covered Withypool Hill above the Barle valley on the left and a shallow farmland valley on the right. For the next mile a gentle climb and a smooth road surface encourage a fast walking pace. At the end of the tarmac, the way becomes a track along the edge of rough land before crossing the road known as Landacre Lane. This leads down to a famous old stone bridge of the same name which can only be seen at a distance on this walk. The route then becomes a stony moorland track. A banked enclosure remains on the left until it turns away down towards the Barle, leaving only heather, grass and bracken on all sides.

At the second of two track junctions on the open moor the way turns left and heads gently downhill towards the Barle at Horsen Ford, a mile and a half away. Withypool Hill, originally on the left, is now behind and has been replaced by the wild empty reaches of Brightworthy Barrows. In the valley bottom beside the winding river there are far fewer trees than before and enclosed land, where it still exists, no longer contains rich green grass. Thus the lush valley below Withypool slowly changes to something very different.

The moor in these parts provides a home for sheep and a herd of Exmoor ponies. The latter are beautiful little animals with sandy russet coats. All ages remain together and also show a marked preference for the track, probably because the grazing is better here. This brings the animals into close contact with humans but their only reaction is a wary eye. This ancient breed is believed to have lived on the moor much longer than man. Through centuries of exposure they have become very hardy, able to forage for themselves and survive outdoors in all weather conditions. Until recent times the breed was an important working animal on many upland farms, carrying country folk on both business and pleasure, hauling traps and carts and has even been known to pull the plough. Their fortunes reached a low ebb after wanton slaughter during the Second World War and for a time it seemed that the tough little breed might be lost. Nowadays, with the preservation of endangered species a priority, their future seems assured.

As the track curves gently down the moor a small conifer plantation comes into view near the ford ahead. Past plans for large conifer forests along the tops of the high moors would have completely spoilt the traditional character of Exmoor but public outcry at the time was able to put an end to the scheme. Here, at the other extreme, a modest group of conifers adds interest without compromising the impact of the wider scene.

Horsen Ford is a lovely lonely place far removed from roads and traffic where the only sounds are of rushing water and the wind in the trees. I have long been aware that away from its few honeypots Exmoor is one of the most tranquil areas of England. Confirmation of this came recently. In 1995 the Council for the Protection of Rural England and the Countryside Commision sponsored a series of 'tranquility' maps for the whole country. These took account of such things as the proximity of towns and settlements, industrial sites, busy roads, railways and airports, airfields, wind power sites and power lines etc. Alas the results were most disappointing. They showed that only three extensive areas of tranquility now remain, upland Northumberland, the Shropshire Marches and, last but by no means least, Exmoor.

'Horsen' is said to be a shortened form of 'Horseham' meaning 'an enclosure for horses' and was probably a place were Exmoor ponies were once collected. Horsen Farm lies out of sight over the brow of the hill to the south where the slopes gain more benefit from the sun. This was one of the local farms established by the Knight family in the nineteenth

The Barle at Horsen Ford

century. Years ago my youngest son and I spent a night at the farm and my lasting impression is of a cold bleak place and of a family who could not have been more welcoming and friendly. Pickedstones, another Knight farm, stands above the conifer trees at the ford. The nearby riverside scene contrasts sharply with the upland hills beyond, especially in late summer when masses of wild montbretia, growing in profusion along the edges of the water, display their orange-red blooms. These flowers presumably escaped from their garden confines long ago and have since more than held their own in this harsh environment.

The walk remains on the Barle's north bank. Above Horsen Ford the valley widens at the junction with White Water. Here the eye is caught by two prominent humps rising from the level valley bottom. The nearer and much smaller of the two is the Calf and the other is Cow Castle. The impact of the latter is heightened by its size and complete detachment from the surrounding valley walls, the latter suggesting that the Barle may have once flowed around its other side. Even today the ground on this dry side is only marginally higher than the river bank. Cow Castle is an excellent natural fortress and it is no surprise to see an Iron Age ditch and rampart around its top. However this place of refuge had one drawback. Any moves by the defenders, unless made in mist or at night would have always been in full view of their enemies on the higher surrounding hills.

Upstream the Barle is again confined to a narrow winding valley but now its steep sides only have a covering of rough grass and bracken. After several twists and turns, bare spoil heaps not yet reclaimed by nature come into view ahead. These are the more obvious remains of Wheal Eliza Mine and close inspection reveals a shaft together with a dry leat and a water wheel pit on the opposite bank of the river. The wheel once powered the pump which kept the mine dry. Further up the track there are vestigial remains of former cottages.

The success of the Brendon Hills iron ore mining ventures in the nineteenth century encouraged similar activity here. Visible evidence of local open cast ore mining during the Middle Ages and possibly long before provided a further spur. The driving force for this latest exploration came from the Knight family, of whom more will be heard later. After much effort and expenditure, both at Wheal Eliza and elsewhere, only limited amounts of ore were found. This particular mine was worked for several years before closing down.

Afterwards the shaft acquired a grisly reputation. It was here that a man named Burgess hid the body of his young daughter after murdering her. Apparently the only reason for his cruel act was that she had become a nuisance to him. He was arrested, confessed to his crime and was subsequently hanged in public at Taunton in 1858.

Winter sunshine, the Barle Valley near Wheal Eliza

Beyond Wheal Eliza the track climbs briefly over a small saddle between the hillock known as Flexbarrow and the main body of higher ground on the north side of the valley. This isolated feature, situated in the middle of a pronounced meander, suggests that before the valley was cut down to its present level the river once took a more direct route across this saddle in circumstances similar to those at Cow Castle. Flexbarrow means 'burial mound beside the stream', a name given in error long ago as there is no evidence of any tomb here. After Flexbarrow the windings of the river become less pronounced and the water alternately flows and then rests for a time in long still pools. The hills above, empty apart from grass, bracken and occasional small bushes, descend to isolated trees beside the water. Further upstream the valley floor widens. With the changes of scene since leaving Withypool the view ahead might have been

The Barle at Flexbarrow

expected to have become even more sparse and harsh. Instead masses of mature trees, mostly beeches, mark the approach to Simonsbath.

Until the Knight family arrived here in the early eighteen hundreds, this part of the valley and all the surrounding hills and moors were almost treeless. They created this attractive change at Simonsbath and also brought about many others to the surrounding countryside, some of which are not so highly regarded by those who love the moors today.

The herculean efforts of the Knights during the 1800s have made them inseparable from today's Exmoor. Their story has every element of a classic tragedy. It can be summed up as setting out with high hopes and great enthusiasm, of tremendous and long lasting efforts and an end in failure.

The Knights were a family of ironmasters from the West Midlands who grew wealthy during the early years of the Industrial Revolution. Latterly they had also gained some knowledge of lowland farming in that region. Like many other successful industrialists of the time, their aim was now to become accepted members of the country's upper class. This could be achieved by using their wealth to purchase or create a large estate around a new or existing mansion which would then provide the base for the dynasty which they hoped would succeed them.

The early nineteenth century was also a time when man held the arrogant belief that, as God's chosen creature, he could and should improve nature by shaping it to meet his own selfish requirements. This was also a time when the country badly needed more arable land to feed its rapidly growing population. Each of these strands played a part in the challenge which the Knight's set for themselves. This was to convert the many square miles of 'waste' within the bounds of the old Exmoor Royal Forest into rich farmland. For centuries this land had been of no interest to royalty and had only been used for rough grazing. Then, when the government of the day finally put the property on the market, John Knight came along and purchased most of it.

54

Bearing in mind the former treeless nature of the terrain, the word 'Forest' might seem puzzling. It comes from the alternative and older meaning of the word describing a part of the country reserved for hunting.

The Knight's ignorance of this high, wet, acid and very windswept terrain was revealed by their initial plans to convert it into arable farmland for grain growing. Once established it was intended that the family, as patrician owners of a vast estate, would then live in a new mansion to be erected at Simonsbath.

Previously there had only been a single rather derelict farm on the site, originally built by James Boevey the Warden of the Royal Forest of Exmoor during the seventeenth century. The Knights moved into this property on what they believed was a temporary basis. In the event it proved to be their one and only Exmoor home.

Much effort and money were put into enclosing the Forest within a stone wall, into providing roads to and from Simonsbath and then into draining, deep ploughing and neutralising the wet acid land. For many years there was little or no financial return. When Frederic Knight took over from his father he made the sensible decision to switch from arable to hill farming. One of his lasting contributions to today's scene is said to be the omnipresent beech windbreaks on top of stone-faced earth banks. He also replaced centralised control of farming from Simonsbath with a landlord-tenant system and most of the farms on the former Royal Forest date from this time.

However problems still abounded. Satisfactory tenants were hard to find and many who took up the challenge soon failed, especially those who had come from more favoured lowland regions. Financial returns remained poor and efforts to improve family fortunes by iron ore mining and other mineral ventures also came to nought.

The beginning of the end came when Frederic's son and heir died at the early age of twenty eight. From that time onwards there were no new ventures, only consolidation of those already started. The mansion at Simonsbath, located behind the present Simonsbath House and known as the Great House, remained a gaunt shell until it was demolished at the end of the nineteenth century. At this time most of the estate was sold to the Fortescue family. Since then large areas have passed into other ownership including, in more recent times, that of the National Park.

Simonsbath also stands astride the Harepath, the prehistoric route across Exmoor from east to west. Legend states that the settlement's name came from a Dane called Sigmund who liked to bathe here. It is also claimed that he helped the native Celts in their efforts to ward off the invading Anglo-Saxons. This seems doubtful because as far as I am aware the Danes only appeared in these parts some two hundred years after the Anglo-Saxons had wrested control from the earlier inhabitants. In addition it is rare to find any historic praise for Danes

Simonsbath House

56

in this part of the country where they are best known as robbing, destroying and raping raiders. Today Simonsbath is a small pleasant well-wooded hamlet with a simple but impressive church, far too large for the present sparse population. The building stands above the road at the top of the settlement and, as might be expected, it was sponsored by the Knights. Frederic Knight's grave stands in a prominent position at the front.

Limited accommodation is available in the village for those who might wish to spend the night here. At one end of the scale there is Simonsbath House, the former home of James Boevey and the Knights, now a hotel, and at the other there is at least one B&B establishment.

⤛ STAGE 7 ⤜

SIMONSBATH TO LYNTON

The walk now heads back over the high moors before dropping down to the coast at Lynmouth. The beautiful and very varied scenery along the way provides full reward for the effort. The highest part of the route, from Preyway Head over Exe Head to Cheriton, is exposed in bad weather.

The typical Exmoor hill has gentle rounded sides beneath a near flat top and is often joined to others of its like, making the beauty of the moors difficult to capture in photographs. In addition local topography is often described by its rivers and streams rather than by its hills. This applies to the present stage.

It starts beside the Barle at Simonsbath and climbs to the infant Exe. From here the route drops to a small stream flowing into Hoaroak Water. Beyond the Hoar Oak the way remains parallel to this river for several miles before crossing at Smallcombe Bridge. The bank of Hoaroak Water is followed down to Hillsford Bridge, followed by a climb to Myrtleberry Cleave high above the confluence of Hoaroak Water and the East Lyn. The route then passes along the lip of the East Lyn Valley before turning into the neighbouring West Lyn Valley. After crossing this river a final climb leads to Lynton.

The starting point is the Exmoor National Park carpark in Simonsbath and already there is an interesting diversion. The substantial Victorian house standing on the main road above the entrance to the carpark is the old rectory. It was built in the 1850s for the first curate of Exmoor, William Thornton.

In the past many fascinating Exmoor folk were illiterate and they have left no record behind. Local priests were an exception, especially during the nineteenth century when most were university graduates from well-off families. However their classics degrees were usually followed by minimal training for the church and at first they must have found it difficult to minister to their often impoverished and illiterate flocks. William Thornton was one such man. He loved physical activity and was headstrong to the point of recklessness. Yet there was a caring streak to his nature and he put great energy into any cause which he thought worthwhile. Rev. Thornton also had an abiding love for Exmoor which he first knew as a student in the 1840s and later as a curate at Lynton in the early 1850s.

He arrived at Simonsbath in 1856, when the Knight's colonisation of the high moor was still under way. This rough and tumble community not only attracted hard workers but also the failures of society. Communications were still poor with the law and other essential services at a distance. In many respects

Simonsbath would have resembled the developing colonial settlements of the same period. Rev.Thornton loved the life here. He could hunt and fish, ride and walk, and on occasion even run considerable distances. From his account he was always dashing to and fro over the moor, seemingly regardless of the need, time of day or weather. Maybe it was the challenge of these journeyings which drove him on.

Some of his scrapes seem foolhardy. Once he was knocked off his horse on Preyway Head in thick snow while attempting to reach Lynmouth for a Christmas dinner and on another he became lost in fog and dark near Simonsbath and drove his horse into a bog. He managed to extricate himself but the animal was not rescued until the following day. Many who love to wander over Exmoor today share most if not all of Rev.Thornton's enthusiasms. Then he got married and that was the beginning of the end. It was difficult to attract servants to Simonsbath and even harder to get them to stay. Food could run short when the inadequate roads were blocked by snow. His wife was lonely and lost her first baby. The doctor was 10 miles away at South Molton and could only be summoned by messenger. Finally Rev.Thornton's father came to the rescue and bought his son the living of a village near Exeter.

The hectic, rough and isolated life of Simonsbath one hundred and fifty years ago is unimaginable in today's peaceful surroundings which, with rapid transport and modern communications, have become a peaceful but integral part of the modern world.

A path leads away from the entry to the upper parking level and passes through trees in the bottom of Ashcombe. Considerable height is then gained climbing three meadows in turn and the surroundings have changed on reaching the small damp dip near the head of this stream. Here the ground cover is coarse and clumps of bog grass thrive in the wettest places. The enclosure above is rough and reverting to moorland. A field gate leads onto the flat hilltop and the route follows the edge of a further enclosure to the road at Preyway Head where, long ago, Rev.Thornton was thrown from his horse into snow. Preyway was the name of the original track between Simonsbath and Lynmouth, later replaced by the Knights' well engineered highway.

In fine weather the views are delightful but if it is bad or visibility poor then there may be little or nothing to see. On the good days the nearby infant Exe appears as a stark empty trough and beyond wonderful rolling grassy slopes, unhindered by fences and enclosures, stretch away to a wide empty horizon. This lovely bleak scene would once have been despised as a filthy barren waste unworthy of God or man but nowadays the inhabitants of a crowded ever busier world have come to love and respect the sanctuary and peace it provides.

I once came along the sweeping tops to the north on a solitary skyline walk which took me all the way from Dunkery Beacon in the east to the end of the moors in the west. The stretch between Warren Farm and Brendon Two Gates proved wilder than expected with glutinous bogs everywhere and no sign of any path, only occasional random animal tracks. At one point I all but trod on a large sleeping fox, much to the great consternation of both of us. After momentary hesitation the animal stood up and loped off at speed while I stood transfixed until it had disappeared. In retrospect I believe that it was the marked similarity between the dangerous lonely sea marshes of my youth and the moors of my adult life that made the latter all the more attractive when I first came upon them.

The rough enclosures on the north side of the infant Exe are a favourite haunt of red deer. Their name is also said to be embodied in that of Dure Down, an area of high ground to the left of the road and the next part of the route. From a layby the way is along a permissive bridleway heading west towards Exe Head.

At first the track is clear cut along the boundary of a high pasture but becomes obscure on entering a wide boggy terrain. The next objective is the track crossing at Exe Head which is set in a slight dip and may be difficult to locate if visibility is poor. At these times it is advisable to set a compass bearing before leaving the end of the recognisable boundary.

River sources, including that of the Exe often disappoint. A short distance from the track junction a trickle of discoloured water slowly oozes from black peaty earth. From here the route follows a well-made track to the north which heads for the deep cleft at the lower end of the Chains Valley. All around gently curving open moorland, covered in lank coarse grass, stretches away unimpeded by man-made boundaries. No doubt wishful thinking once encouraged me to believe that this was virgin wilderness but I was puzzled by knowledge that extensive heather moorland existed a few miles away. Now I know that the coexistence of separate heather and grass moors in this high country is the result of different land management practices in the past.

The slow growing dip on the right may mark the burgeoning River Exe but it is the steep sided valley immediately ahead which holds the eye. This leads to Hoaroak Water, one of the main tributaries of the West Lyn. The source of the Barle is also two miles away above Pinkery Pond, so the three largest rivers of Exmoor rise close together. This high damp area includes the notorious Chains, the source of the Lynmouth flood disaster in 1952. On that occasion very heavy rain on top of moors already sodden by previous downpours made every stream and river a murderously destructive torrent, aggravated on the Lyn by its steep and narrow valley sides.

The valley bottom ahead falls away rapidly and, as the track at first descends slowly, the two become separated by a steep drop. Track and water are finally reunited far below where Hoaroak Water, descending from the Chains, enters from the left. Ahead a high bluff with the remains of a building on top overlook the valley bottom. The scene reminds me of the ruins of a tribal fort commanding a mountainous pass but the map says that it is only a prosaic sheepfold. If so it was a windy exposed choice.

The valley eventually widens and the famous Hoar Oak comes into view on the right. Trees were once few in these parts and solitary specimens often provided convenient boundary markers. A predecessor of the present oak on the same spot marked the boundary of the old royal hunting forest. Close by John Knight's enclosing stone wall straddles hills and valleys for almost thirty miles.

The walk turns away from the track, crosses the stream, which might be difficult in spate, and climbs to the Hoar Oak. At the tree the route turns left and on passing through a gate in the wall leaves the old Exmoor Royal Forest and Knight Country behind.

The abandoned Hoar Oak Farm is on the left, its meadows invaded by bracken and former hedge boundaries grown into straggles of mature beeches. The way ahead lies along the side of a lovely heather, bracken and grass covered slope where each species forever fights for more than its fair share of soil and sun. Here on a fine day there is no better place in the world to be, yet few come this way.

At the start the path is obscure but on reaching the top of Cheriton Ridge it becomes a broad green track along the undulating crest. At first there are no signs of enclosed land. Then it appears far away on both sides. Little by little the encroaching boundaries close in until, at the end, the remaining moor is a narrow funnel pointing towards a field gate. The ground has also undergone a marked change, now resembling a well cropped meadow. Occasional foraging sheep along the way have also grown to a large number. From the field gate a stony track leads to a narrow lane which is followed past Scoresdown Farm, the first nearby inhabited dwelling seen for many miles. The way then dwindles to a rough narrow track heading downhill into Hoar Oak Valley.

The steep valley walls are now well wooded, mostly with native trees. Hoar Oak Water is crossed at Smallcombe Bridge and the route turns right onto a path through trees beside the river. Convenient riverside seats provide a good place to stop, sit and listen to the song of the water passing along the fully fledged river. This new idyll is both a short distance and yet a world away from the former wide empty moorland.

After crossing a meadow and passing a small carpark, the route emerges onto the road at Hillsford Bridge. The sound, sight and smell of traffic is an unpleasant shock after the peace and purity of the open moor. Fortunately the distance is short, at the first bend on the climb the road is exchanged for a peaceful path heading gently upwards through trees.

Hoaroak Water near the Hoar Oak

A substantial Iron Age earthwork appears ahead, apparently a settlement not a fort. However in times of need the former inhabitants might have been able to retreat to the massive fortification known as Wind Hill, only a mile to the north but on the other side of the East Lyn River.

As the track climbs and veers to the west the view opens out and becomes dramatic. To the front massive Hollerday Hill towers above the seashore and far below a deep wooded ravine traces the winding course of the East Lyn back to its confluence with Hoar Oak Water. This new mountainous scene is very different from the worn-down gentle Exmoor hills seen so far along the way. The new dynamic surroundings are the result of a tumultuous and relatively recent geological event. It seems that at one time the two Lyn rivers flowed at a much higher level than today and their combined course, after passing through the site of present day Lynton, went on to meet the sea somewhere to the west.

There are two theories about the change. One is that a combination of sea and river erosion broke through the original north wall of the Lyn Valley above the present site of Lynmouth. This created a much lower river bed which soon cut steep-sided valleys back into the hills, with the remaining part of the original river valley left high and dry at present day Lynton and in the Valley of Rocks.

The other theory is that a massive ice wall pushed against the present coast during the Ice Ages and caused the rivers to overflow temporarily through Lynton to the west. The first theory is the favoured one and given today's dramatic scene one can still picture the 500 foot high waterfall that would have been created when the valley wall was first breached. The water erosion which caused massive changes in the past still continues today through a combination of steady flow and brief violent events. The last tumultuous torrent occurred within living memory. In 1952 Lynmouth was struck by a mass of water and tumbling rocks and 34 people lost their lives. At the time of my first visit in 1951, Lynmouth was still a quaint unchanged Victorian resort and I was very much taken with it. On returning many years later I had difficulty in relating some of my memories to the modern scene due to changes. In particular I have never been able to trace the little guest house beside the river where I stayed. After the flood many badly damaged properties were demolished, a new highway was created and the lower reaches of the river were widened and diverted around the harbour.

The path eventually leaves the high ground at Myrtleberry Cleave to zig zag down to a small stream before climbing again to the top of Lyn Cleave. In this dip I once encountered an adder basking in the warm sun of an early autumn day before it awoke, took fright and hastily slithered away. By now a growing sound like that of the windswept sea emanates from the turbulent East Lyn far below as it crashes into rocks all the way down to the shore.

The spectacular viewpoint on Lyn Cleave is known as Summer House Hill. Below rock outcrops protrude from the steep hillside and across a void the East Lyn pours through seemingly tiny trees. Further away the clustered buildings of Lynmouth cling to narrow spaces along the river and shore, a great crescent of rock debris reaches out into the Bristol Channel, Lynton perches on its high shelf half way up to the tops and higher still Hollerday Hill, a great bulk of rock, stands above Lynton and hangs over both Lynmouth and the sea.

Summer House Hill is named after a summerhouse which once stood here. A popular old print shows the Bristol Channel full of sailing ships, some with ancillary steam power. Not only has the summerhouse gone but the sea is now all but empty of vessels. Some buildings at Lynton and Lynmouth are recognisable but many new ones have been added as well as bridges, roads and prominent car parks. However nature, in the form of thick woodland covering the hills, still appears much the same. The part of the summerhouse shown in the print is flimsy, the rough-hewn pillars and roof timbers no doubt explaining its total absence from the scene today.

The splendid views are left behind as the path turns inland and drops down through trees into the West Lyn valley. Half a mile further on the sound of rushing water grows to a roar and Lyn Bridge appears, a mountainous place where buildings both overhang the turbulence and cling to the steep hillside above.

The name 'Lyn' derives from the old English word 'Hlynn' meaning 'torrent' and it could not be more appropriate. The West Lyn, a rushing mass of white water, descends more than 1500 feet in 4 miles. From here the way ahead is across the main road and along a narrow lane heading diagonally up the hill in the direction of the sea. The lane narrows to a path passing isolated buildings on the steep hillside before arriving at the compact centre of Lynton.

Lynton and Lynmouth developed together in the nineteenth century. There was more space for building up here and the original hamlet soon grew into a large Victorian village. At Lynmouth the dramatic scenery dominates everything. By contrast all is completely hidden from view at Lynton's centre, even Hollerday Hill appearing as a modest rise. Lynton was not affected by the 1951 flood disaster and its Victorian features have remained intact. One stands out from the rest. This is the town hall which, while displaying a wild mix of medieval and Tudor styling, clearly cannot be anything other than the creation of its own time. It was donated to the community by George Newnes, the publisher and local benefactor in 1900.

FROM LYNTON TO LYNMOUTH VIA THE HEDDON VALLEY

The countryside and coast to the west of Lynton are outstanding, very different from Exmoor's other more subdued attractions. This stage is also more challenging than most.

The route is circular, with the outward leg inland and the return along the coast. Although the two are never far apart, their immediate surroundings and wider views are often very different.

This walk is longer than most. It will also take more time to complete than might be anticipated as there are many ups and downs, numerous points of interest and in addition wayfinding needs some care.

Starting from Lynton church, the walk heads past shops and the town hall before turning left along one of several cross streets to Lydiate Lane, a main road out of the village. Lydiate Lane climbs and soon reaches a corner where it doubles back uphill. Here the route continues ahead up a narrow lane to a small agricultural yard and the start of a path enclosed by trees and bushes.

The Victorian townscape in the valley has so far given no hint of the nearby spectacular scenes. Hollerday Hill seems no more than a modest rise above the rooftops and there is no sign of the sea. Now, enclosed by foliage, all distant views have gone. A small quarry is passed by and at a fork the route turns left.

The climb continues until the trees fall behind. Although not visible from here, the lip of the slope above marks the start of meadows undulating away to the south. The valley and path veer to the north and a rocky hillside appears ahead. Then at a high corner, where the valley swings back to the west, rocky hills rising to pinnacles, a rugged coast and the wide sea come into view all at once. The effect is stunning.

This part of the Exmoor coast is unique. As stated earlier, the River Lyn once flowed through Lynton and the valley below, entering the sea somewhere to the west. Although the most significant break in the valley's north wall occured at Lynmouth, there are signs of others in the immediate scene in the form of breaks in the line of rocky pinnacles tumbling into the sea. At the eastern end Hollerday Hill reduces to a pinnacle ridge above the Valley of Rocks and after a break the huge stones of Castle Rock reach up to the sky. Further west, another break at Wringcliff Bay is followed by rugged Duty Point hill. Beyond lies Lee Bay and then Crock Point, which bears some resemblance to a child's

Castle Rock from the zig-zag path below South Cleave

playground slide and may be the last isolated remnant of the former valley floor. From here the scene to the west becomes more typical of the Exmoor coast, with high hills falling directly into the sea.

More rocks are visible in the immediate vicinity than anywhere else on Exmoor. Bronze Age peoples lived on both Dartmoor and Exmoor and on the former, encouraged by many naturally occurring boulders, they built circles, standing stones, processional ways and tombs. It seems likely that they constructed the same here. Although nothing is visible today, nineteenth century reports indicate that there were once several stone circles in the central part of this valley and that these 'Druidic Remains' were later broken up and the most suitable stones sold off as gate posts. However old prints only show many random stones standing and lying around on the valley floor. Since then much of this ground has been cleared and enclosed.

The Cheesering

Further along, as the hillside and path follow the twists and turns of the valley, Lee Abbey comes into view. Set in the valley bottom where the meadows fall away more steeply to the west, the Abbey looks out on a wonderful panorama of hills, cliffs and sea. Unfortunately this motley collection of buildings is itself far from wonderful. The unpleasant impact it creates might not have been as marked in a less attractive region but here it is a blot on one of the country's most beautiful landscapes.

Lee Abbey was not a genuine abbey but a house built in Victorian times on the site of Lee Farm. The

Crock Point

67

original building, much smaller than today's conglomeration, had mock Tudor features and a gatehouse. Old photos reveal its romantic appeal but even this structure is said to have caused a great outcry at the time. If so one can hardly imagine the protesters' reaction to today's eyesore.

After passing through a small area of moorland, the path enters a long downhill zig zag. The end of the zig presents fine views of nearby Castle Rock and the steep tree covered hillside to the west which descends in a graceful curve to the meadows on the valley floor. The path drops down into these trees. Then, when the foliage becomes thick, there is no more sky, sea, meadows or even Lee Abbey. The near-level track contours across the lower hillside, at one point crossing a little stream hurtling down a very steep slope.

Bonhill Bridge is a mile away to the south-west up a long narrow valley and the stream from this valley is encountered next. After crossing a wooden footbridge and mounting the steps beyond, the route turns left onto a track leading to the bridge. The surrounding woods are mostly of oak and beech but stands of pine and larch grow among them. Further along there are slender meadows in the valley bottom now showing signs of neglect. If continued these will soon become part of the surrounding woodland. Most of England was covered by a thick blanket of trees before the first farmers arrived more than four thousand years ago and given the opportunity these native woods would very soon extend all the way across the country once again.

The track goes over Bonhill Bridge and past the nearby lonely cottage. Trees continue on the left but the hillside on the right is now a meadow. Croscombe Barton, an attractive large stone house with attendant outbuildings appears in the valley bottom ahead. At the entrance a sign invites walkers to take an alternative path avoiding the disused farmyard. This crosses a bridge over the now small stream but then makes a long detour to the north before returning to the public footpath. From here the route heads west over further meadows before entering the highway at Slattenslade.

At Slattenslade the lane is followed westwards for a mile up to the small village of Martinhoe. Along the way there is a striking rearward view of the land dropping steeply into the sea, with the dry valley, Duty Point and Castle Rock all very prominent.

Modern Martinhoe is a spick and span hamlet with an attractive small church, very different from the old days when the settlement would have been more populous and much less affluent. Parts of the church date from the eleventh century and the tower resembles a fortress with narrow slits for windows.

Pirates attacked this lonely coast right up to the seventeenth century and the tower was probably a refuge for the villagers. A number of stones with epitaphs to the Ridd family stand close to the graveyard entrance. These include more than one John Ridd and even a Lorna Doone Ridd.

Many notable men would have served this church over the years but today the best known dates from the nineteenth century. James Hannington was the curate in 1874. A decade later he became the first bishop of Eastern Equatorial Africa where he is said to have interpreted his duties rather broadly. A short time later he led an expedition into the interior and was murdered by the natives. This act is believed to have been carried out at the behest of the King of Uganda who thought Hannington's missionary work was undermining his authority. The lane turns away from the coast to run parallel to the deep wooded trench of the Heddon Valley on the right, backed by the final western heather-clad bastions of Exmoor, Trentishoe Down, Holdstone Down and distant Great Hangman.

The last looms above the ocean and at 1050 feet is the highest English hill falling directly into the sea. This is the only view of the scene as the walk's western turning point is now at hand. The road verge broadens and a footpath on the right descends along the edge of a meadow, then through bushes and trees, to Mannnacott Farm. From here the route enters a lane heading into the Heddon Valley. The climate is lush in the upper reaches of this valley. Vigorous trees grow along its sides and there are green meadows in the bottom. The Hunter's Inn is the focal point and when I first came walking through the valley in 1951, my friend and I stopped here for a midday meal. For us at the time, as we munched a hot lunch in the otherwise deserted dining room, it was an unprecedented expensive event. My diary states that this 'was a large hotel of the type built during the inter-War years', an observation which has not stood the test of time. I would no longer consider the building large and have since discovered that it replaced an earlier one burnt down at the end of the nineteenth century.

The previous building may have started life as a simple wayside inn but by the time a chimney spark set fire to the thatched roof it had already been expanded to accommodate an early form of tourism. Oxford University reading parties stayed here. In the very remote peaceful surroundings of the time, well-to-do young men would have been seen lounging around with their heads buried in works of classical Greek and Latin. Today's scene is very different. A carpark, public toilets and a National Trust shop have now been added for the benefit of the numerous and often lively holidaymakers who arrive here on foot and by car.

The Hunter's Inn is the most westerly point of the walk and there is now a choice of ways forward, both starting on the right of the inn. One is a path and the other an old carriage drive. The path joins the South West Coast Path which becomes a mountainous traverse above the sea and the drive, for those who might prefer something less dramatic, follows the hillside up to Woody Bay. On reaching Woody Bay the lane is then followed downhill to rejoin the South West Coast Path continuing eastwards.

Exmoor's Western Coast

The path, the most pleasurable alternative, at first winds through trees beside the rushing river. Both climate and vegetation change along the way. Trees become small and then are replaced by bracken, grass, heather and occasional small clumps of gorse. The yellow blossom of the last provides pleasure all summer long and well into the autumn. There are two bridges along the way, a new stone one, carrying the Coast Path from the west and a wooden footbridge further down.

A detour to Heddon's Mouth is highly recommended. For this the river should be crossed and its west bank followed down to the sea. The valley sides are now covered in raw scree and at the Mouth the river runs onto a lonely beach bounded by ferocious rocks and cliffs. The only obvious sign of man is an

The Old Lime Kiln, Heddon's Mouth

old ruined lime kiln once served by sailing vessels. Past travellers have likened the kiln to a castle guarding the shore and perhaps this is what it should have been. For a long time pirates landed here and the beach was also used by smugglers. More recently it is said that crews of U-boats, preying on British shipping during World War Two, also landed here to replenish vital stocks of fresh water. From the beach the Coast Path heading eastwards is visible high above, climbing towards the seaward cliffs.

Steps are now retraced to the Coast Path heading east. A steady climb across areas of scree leads to Highveer Point, a massive buttress of rugged rock which provides a magnificent viewing platform. Here the dramatic north coast, extending both east and west, comes into view for the first

Approaching Woody Bay on the South West coast path

time. On sunny days the high mountainous cliffs, dark in shadow, etch brutal outlines onto the blue sea far below: an awesome scene which can never be erased from memory. Beyond the Point the path continues eastwards, looping from outcrop to outcrop across the face of a steep heather-covered slope above the sea. This path is well made and secure but should not be attempted in rough weather. While here it is difficult to appreciate that the intimate domesticity of pretty little Martinhoe is only a short distance away and high above.

The remains of Hannington's Path are somewhere nearby, the selfsame man who was the curate at Martinhoe. While at university, he had stayed at Martinhoe Vicarage as a member of a reading party. It seems that instead of studying he explored the cliffs below the village and then constructed a path down to some caves near the shore. His hired labour gave up when the rock turned out to be rotten and he finished the task with only the vicar's son for help. As might be expected Hannington later had some difficulty in obtaining his degree. It is also clear that his zeal for hazardous challenges never waned and in the end was to cost him dear.

The path passes a final rock outcrop and then heads into a small combe where the Hollow Brook, the small stream from Martinhoe, falls to the shore in a series of cascades ending in a waterfall 230 feet high. It resembles the streams in faraway Norway which cascade down the mountain sides into fjords.

Bushes now crowd in both sides and increase to mature trees on turning the corner into Woody Bay. The wider scene across the water encompasses a wooded hillside pierced by occasional buildings, the more distant tortured rocks of Crock Point and beyond the pinnacles and cliffs leading to the heights of Hollerday Hill. The path then enters a track leading to several Woody Bay homes and becomes submerged in trees.

At a junction near a small dwelling, the track heads down to the shore and the Coast Path narrows. If time and energy permit a detour down to the beach is well worthwhile. However significant height has to be regained on the way back and there are no facilities of any sort down at the bay.

The track to the shore weaves downhill through woodland, crossing a small stream which finally emerges as a waterfall onto the beach. The thick foliage of summer months restricts distant views but occasional glimpses of the sea surface reveal the extent of descent remaining. Beyond the last isolated dwelling the track becomes a rock paved path winding past an old lime kiln down to the beach.

Woody Bay is a place which puts its own special stamp on the mind. Behind a shore interspersed with rocks and huge boulders, a massive near-vertical cliff rears up to distant trees. In other parts similar trees reach almost down to the water. The eastern limits of the bay are marked by distant Crock Point, much lower than the immediate surroundings but composed of impressive rugged rocks.

The high ground behind the bay permits little sunlight to enter its confines, increasing the pervasive solitude to a point where it verges on sadness and secrecy. Past events not only leave their physical mark on a place but also remain part of its atmosphere. This is so here, for the bay has had its misfortunes.

For a long time little occurred. Access to the beach by sea and from it by land were both difficult but a lime kiln was built to improve the soil of the meadows above. Then at the end of the nineteenth century an entrepreneur planned to develop Woody Bay into a resort competing with nearby Lynton and Lynmouth. Roads were laid out and a hotel and villas built. The focal point of the scheme was a tall steamer pier projecting 70 yards offshore which would provide berthing at all stages of the tide. In addition it was proposed to connect Woody Bay to the then newly completed narrow gauge railway between Barnstaple and Lynton. Disaster was not long in coming. The jetty was badly damaged in a storm shortly after completion, the project then failed and the promoter was later sent to prison for misappropriating his backers' funds. On reflection this very enclosed steep spot would hardly be a suitable location for

Crock Point and Duty Point from Woody Bay

a popular coastal resort. The next proprietor wished to make Woody Bay a private place and attempted to exclude all transient visitors. This led to a court case for obstructing a public footpath. Fortunately for society at large much of Woody Bay is now in the care of the National Trust.

After climbing back to the meeting of ways, the route turns left along the Coast Path which eventually emerges onto a narrow coast road. Unfortunately the South West Coast Path is obliged to follow this highway for the next 2 miles. The ascent of the tall cliff seen from the bay is disappointing because, enclosed by dense foliage, it allows no view and no hint of height gained. If an attempt is made to peer through any small gap in foliage, it is likely that a vehicle will come nudging up. The often busy road is very narrow and in places walkers are obliged to press into the bank to make way for passing vehicles.

From the top the road descends past Crock Point, named after the nearby Crock Pits. Dutch entrepreneurs quarried pottery clay here during the eighteenth century for shipment back to the Netherlands. At the bottom a little valley leads to Lee Bay and the carpark here can be busy during the holiday season. The next stretch of road is unpleasant. The steady climb along a narrow, fenced and often busy highway permits no enjoyment of the splendid all round views. Sight of the lovely but very private path next to the sea at Duty Point makes the effort even more irksome. Most of today's public paths around the coast were originally excisemen's patrol routes and Duty Point's name tends to suggest that this was so here. If correct the path could have been lost to the public when Lee Abbey was built in the nineteenth century.

The immediate surroundings improve beyond the Lee Abbey estate lodge, changing to unspoilt coastal moorland. Rocks protrude from the steep hillside on the right dominated by the tall stone pillar known as the Cheesering. Castle Rock stands on the left, its boulder strewn slopes leading up to a massive rock bastion. At one special spot beside the lane the White Lady is in view. Below the summit of Castle Rock one boulder leans against another, revealing a patch of sky. From the one special position the patch takes on the shape of a lady wearing a hooded cloak and carrying something, possibly a baby, in her arms. Yet only a few steps away on each side the same shape becomes nondescript. I once came this way on a bad autumn day when very few other people were around. Dark glowering clouds immediately above made every rock in the nearby scene appear black in contrast with the bright sky still lingering out over the sea.

On that occasion the nearby gloom and the distant light produced a White Lady more brilliant than I have ever seen before or since. It was a sight well worth the wetting from the sky which followed. The stark scene on that day reminded me of frightening Old Testament paintings and the thought crossed my mind that the wealthy people who came here in Victorian times, to admire and to be awed by the local scenery, would have been more than rewarded on a day such as this.

The rough hewn path to the top of Castle Rock provides another short very worthwhile detour. I have read somewhere that it was constructed by an old man in the early days of Lynton's tourist trade so that he and his wife could dispense hot water and picnic provisions from a small hut at the top. Commercial activity ceased long ago but the way to the summit remains a great attraction for the many who now come this way. On approaching the top the rocks announce both their massive size and, in contradiction, seem suspended in space above the sea. The views of sea and land from this lofty perch are splendid but it is not a place to dally on a cold wet windy day.

The gap between Castle Rock and the next rugged hill to the east marks the entry to one of the locality's special attractions, the North Walk, a broad tarmac path which crosses the steep seaward side of Hollerday Hill. This hogs-back hill is the most impressive of many along the Exmoor coast. It appears that a line of massive cliffs once faced the sea here. These were later ground down by the scouring action of the frost and ice of the Ice Ages to their present smooth steep profiles. In geological terms the sea has returned only recently and so far has only been able to gnaw new small cliffs and caves at their feet.

The North Walk was constructed as a commercial venture in 1817. The visitors of the time may well have come to experience the savageries of nature but not to clamber up, down and across precipitous slopes, especially the ladies who were badly hampered by their bulky clothes and long skirts. Thus the North Walk, with its broad gently sloping path equipped with convenient bowers and seating places, provided an ideal compromise. Here sauntering ladies and their attendants could, with very little effort, enjoy a trio of visual delights, distant seascapes, dizzy drops and soaring rocky heights. For many years these hills have been home to a succession of feral goats. When visible they can provide a dramatic sight standing four square on lofty rocks. More often than not they remain hidden and then only the more enduring signs of their presence are visible, scattered in the bowers and along the path.

As the path curves around the hill the view of the coast to the west slips behind the nearby slope and the Foreland, a great bulk of rock projecting out to sea, looms into view ahead, the cliffs at its feet climbing to precipitous shallow combes which lead up to gentle rounded tops. The first building of Lynton appears below. The path becomes a track and then a lane. Hotels now stand above and below. At the end the route turns right along the lane into Lynton or left down the zig zag path to Lynmouth, crossing the cliff railway twice on the way.

Approaching Lynton along the North Walk

⇥ STAGE 9 ⇤

LYNMOUTH TO PORLOCK

This stage follows the high coast from Lynmouth to Porlock and there is much beauty, variety and interest along the way.

Although the stage is not over long, numerous ups and downs make it rather demanding. In addition there are three fascinating detours which require significant deviations from the Coast Path. Consequently it may be advantageous to split this stage into two with the break at County Gate. Buses call here regularly during the summer months.

On the way up to Countisbury

PART ONE

My fondness for Lynmouth is such that I am always reluctant to leave. On our last morning in the village in 1951, as my friend and I were about to set out for llfracombe, we both agreed that it would be a good place for a honeymoon. I did not meet the girl I was to marry for several years and, as our wedding was in midwinter, the village did not even get a passing thought. However through a long chain of events linked back to the 1951 visit, my daughter did have part of her's here.

The centre of Lynmouth is busy during the holiday season but, in Exmoor fashion, peace and quiet are only a short step away. The walk, which follows the South West Coast Path, takes the footbridge over the River Lyn to Rock Cottage and then crosses the public park beyond. This greensward is the only extensive area of level ground in the village and was originally part of the river delta which now extends far out to sea. On the left a line of stakes marks the channel through the shingle to the tiny harbour and on the right, across a long narrow sandy bay, the high mass of the Foreland, the centrepiece of the Exmoor coast, dominates both sea and sky.

At the final building beside the shore the route turns uphill, passing a shady leafy glade which becomes a brilliant azure carpet when masses of bluebells appear each spring. A quarter mile climb through trees leads to the main road up Countisbury Hill. Walkers were once obliged to tramp along the busy tarmac but now their lot is much improved with a path along the seaward parapet. At the end of the trees the path leaves the road and heads away across a steep open hillside above the sea.

The massive bulk of the Foreland looms ever larger and far below long narrow Sillery Sands stretch away to the crags and rocks at its outermost point. During the climb the path crosses the remains of an ancient earthwork extending down the precipitous hillside. This was the curtain wall of the large and very impressive Iron Age fort on the top of Wind Hill above. At the end of the climb the little hamlet of Countisbury comes into view. Its church, standing above the other buildings, crouches in a shallow dip to gain some protection from the elements. On approach the fabric of the building may seem very old but this is a measure of a century of weather beatings.

Farewell to Lynton and Lynmouth

79

Countisbury Church appearing through the sea mist

The time has come for a final farewell to Lynmouth and Lynton, now away across the water, the former overshadowed by the bulk of Hollerday Hill and the latter perched on a crowded shelf of land half way up to the tops. Set in a scene of sea, sky and high steep hills, the seemingly tiny buildings define the scale of the whole, providing a picture postcard view which has travelled the world.

The Wind Hill fortification stands on the left of this scene. The site is large and with an adequate number of defenders would have been near impregnable. Inland the ground drops steeply into the East Lyn Valley and on the right precipitously into the sea. The third side faces Countisbury and, although this slope is far from gentle, it is guarded by a massive linear earthwork with a single entrance. Even after more than two thousand years of weathering and without the wooden palisade which once stood on top, it would still make a daunting sight facing an enemy. The fort's size hints at former importance but very little is known about its prehistory.

However if this hill was once known as Arx Cynuit, and the description fits, then it first came into written history in the Anglo-Saxon Chronicles. These state

80

Last glimpse of Lynton

that 23 shiploads of Scandinavian raiders from Wales landed here and the local Anglo-Saxons took up a defensive position in a fort which was already ancient even in their day. Then, taking their enemies by surprise, the defenders rushed out and attacked. The Chronicles state that the Danes' leader, Hubba, and 800 of his men were killed. If true it would seem likely that rather more than 23 ships would have been involved. Danish defeats are a constant legendary theme in this part of the country and both Battlegore at nearby Williton and Dowsborough on the Quantock Hills are associated with similar tales. Taking them as a whole they neither fit the known facts of the Danish incursions nor seem credible bearing in mind their military prowess. I have a theory that actual events were exaggerated afterwards, at a time when the Anglo-Saxons needed to boost flagging morale by putting a rosy glow on their predecessors' achievements. That time might well have been after the humiliating Norman Conquest and during the centuries of oppression which followed.

As a native of part of the old Danelaw where the majority of local place names are Danish, I find it rather sad that these people, nowadays popularly known as Vikings, are only remembered for their misdeeds. During brutal times their behaviour was no worse and often better than that of many of their contemporaries. The facts that they settled peacefully in a large part of England, were rapidly assimilated into the local population, were very law abiding and had a major impact on the developing English nation are nowadays largely unrecognised. The Danes also made a major contribution to our language and introduced the concepts of both trial by a jury of equals and every person as a free citizen. Unfortunately both of the last were badly eroded in later feudal times. It is no accident that the modern English words 'law', 'byelaw' and 'hustings' are all of old Danish origin.

Out on Butter Hill beyond Countisbury the surroundings are bare and very exposed. When strong winds blow off the sea the accompanying near-horizontal rain is most wetting. At other times the high hill is shrouded in mist, the result of humid sea air colliding with its bulk and then rising, cooling and condensing. Then Lynmouth may bask in sunshine but up here thick near-impenetrable grey is only relieved by a glimpse through thinning wraithes to a tantalising shining blue sea below.

Fortunately the time on this exposed top is brief because the Foreland soon reveals that it is not the solid block of rock suggested by the view on the way up. A deep combe can now be seen descending to the east and this is where the walk goes. Coddow Combe has wild steep sides and heads down to the lighthouse road, a narrow winding track through impressive spaces to the end of the land where lighthouse men and their families once lived. The walk follows the road inland and upwards for a short distance to a hilltop. There the coast to the east comes into view. A long line of wooded hogs-backs, tumbling into the sea, extends away to distant Hurlstone Point. Periodic sightings of the last will provide a measure of progress during the hours ahead.

The narrow path now winds across steep wooded hillsides high above the sea, through another of Exmoor's lovely lonely places where pervasive isolation distances the busy outside world. At one spot there is virgin rock but mostly the ground is covered by sessile oaks, birches, rowans and an occasional holly bush.

The path dips in and out a succession of tiny combes cut deep into the rock, each with a little fast stream flowing through its bottom. Born on the moors and woods above, these waters often travel no more than a mile to end on the rocky shore below. Two of the valleys along this way, Glenthorne and Culbone, are larger than most and have provided a home for man.

The foreland from the wooded cliffs to the east

Ahead Old Burrow Hill, tall and crowned with conifers, marks the approach to the Glenthorne Estate and rhododendrons are appearing. These natives of Turkey have taken to these moist acid hillsides with zeal and are now a menace. Although admired for their colourful springtime blossoms, they tolerate no other vegetation and the sterile ground beneath their massed evergreen leaves provides no home for wildlife. For some distance the path becomes a deep trench cut through a dense rhododendron forest. Further along decorative pines, a small grotto and a stone seat confirm the proximity of Glenthorne. Then the path suddenly emerges onto the main drive which zig zags from the coast road down to Glenthorne House. When Rev. W. S. Halliday arrived here in the early part of the nineteenth century, with a substantial legacy in his pocket and notions of creating a romantic estate, these surroundings were only known to itinerant charcoal burners and occasional smugglers. Rev. Halliday had considered several sites around England but the wild scenery of this place and perhaps the challenges it posed won him over.

The route turns up the drive to the lodge which is situated half way along its length. This is a pretty little place, built in what could be described as a Victorian decorative country cottage style. It is also very isolated and the dogs make a great fuss when anyone passes by. The outstanding feature of the spot is the pair of pillars, each surmounted by stone boar's head, which flank the drive.

Beyond the lodge the Coast Path heads away into a dip but the first detour, to the site of the Roman fort on top of Old Burrow Hill, continues upwards along the drive for a further half mile to a point where the conifers on the right are replaced by a sheep meadow enclosed by a wire fence. This is entered through a field gate and the Roman Fort stands on the skyline above.

Two concentric banks and ditches, with their entrances at opposite ends, protect the heart of the encampment. It was constructed during the first century AD, shortly after the West of England had been conquered but before the aggressive Silures of South Wales had succumbed. Thus the northern flank of the Romans' latest acquisition was vulnerable to seaborne attack and this combined lookout and signal station was established to maintain contact with their fleet patrolling the Bristol Channel.

The soldiers occupying this chilly exposed site were apparently obliged to live in leather tents for the whole of their three or four years' stay. After that time the Roman Fort at Martinhoe further to the west was manned until South Wales came under the control of the Roman Legion based at Caerleon. The Old Burrow site is particularly interesting because nothing has changed here since the Romans went away and consequently the site has remained in a pristine state.

Even now, nearly two thousand years on, one can still sense the isolation of the soldiers based in this inhospitable place, far removed from the support of

One of the Boars' Heads at Glenthorne Lodge

Cross at the Sisters' Fountain

their own kind. One can also imagine their feelings of vulnerability as they clustered around their camp fires on cold dark misty nights, always conscious of the potential threats lurking in the large world beyond their dim lights.

The South West Coast Path can be rejoined by taking a path down the combe below the fort to the spot where trees and bushes begin. The Sisters' Fountain is here, its most prominent feature a stone cross mounted on a dome of the rocks.

The marble water trough below is said to have come from one of the Greek Islands and further down a hydraulic ram may clank intermittently. It is a gloomy place, especially on dull wet days, engendering thoughts of a remote wayside burial and seems an odd means of honouring a group of ladies.

It is said that Rev. Halliday made his final decision to build Glenthorne while pondering here and in more recent times the site has become associated with a legend about Jesus.

The Coast Path then follows a track through conifer plantations, bypassing the heart of the Glenthorne Estate. The second recommended detour begins here, down a track signposted to Glenthorne Beach. This passes Home Farm which was erected in 1829 and seems too imposing for the limited amount of farming possible in this steep-sided wooded valley. Some adjoining pigsties and cow sheds are said to have been swept away by the nearby stream at the time of the Lynmouth flood disaster.

Beyond the minuscule fields there is a glimpse of the roofs, pinnacles and mock Tudor chimneys of Glenthorne House. The original name of the locality was Coscombe and Rev. Halliday changed it to Glenthorne, the 'valley of the thorns'.

'Glen' is a Scottish word foreign to the South West and may have come from his northern ancestry or an affection for Sir Walter Scott's Waverley novels which were immensely popular at the time.

The track joins another and curves out onto the shore at Glenthorne Beach. Crowded trees are replaced by a stony beach, an artificial waterfall, wide empty

Glenthorne Beach

waters, distant Hurlstone Point peeping around nearby cliffs and a faraway panorama of the Welsh coast.

Following the smugglers' example, stores and coal for the estate were once brought in by sea. Sailing vessels made a tricky landfall onto this exposed beach and, after grounding, were unloaded by hand at low tide, not a task to undertake with bad weather in the offing! A shipment of coal, delivered in 1929, is the last known cargo.

Even today few people find their way here. Given the surroundings and the solitude, it is not surprising that this lonely spot has acquired a legend. The boy Jesus and his uncle, Joseph of Arimathea, are said to have landed here while on the way to Glastonbury. They were seeking a supply of fresh water but meeting with no success Jesus caused a spring to arise which not only met their needs but still flows today. Unfortunately this story has no historic provenance. The tale of Joseph and the flowering thorn at Glastonbury, in spite of doubtful authenticity, is well documented from medieval times onwards but there is nothing similar about Jesus, Joseph and Glenthorne. This story is modern.

Following these fascinating time-consuming diversions, it may now be time to walk up Yenworthy Combe to the Pinetum and then on through the higher reaches of Glenthorne Estate to County Gate where, during the summer months, there is a daily bus service to Lynmouth and Minehead.

If the diversion down to the beach has been omitted, the continuing Coast Path leads directly to Yenworthy Combe and its small stream which is close to the Pinetum. Of the Pinetum's many tall trees, the highest is a Sequoia Wellingtonia which reaches a height of 98 feet. When planted most were new arrivals from their native lands and Rev. Halliday may have seen them as a means of introducing the wide world into his new domain. Trees grow well here. The site is moist and damp, protected from frosts by the nearby sea and from the prevailing south-westerly gales by the north facing slopes above. Nowadays the site may be less tidy than it was in Rev. Halliday's time, when money was readily available and labour cheap, but it is a pity that he could not have seen it in today's glory.

PART TWO

The South West Coast Path now continues along the high coast from Glenthorne to Porlock Weir before heading through woods to Porlock. Numerous ups and downs still remain. If the stage has been split into two then the second half will be joined after returning from County Gate to Yenworthy Combe.

From the small Yenworthy stream the Coast Path now climbs the east side of the combe, leaving the valleys and woods of Glenthorne at a gate. Once more the path heads through massed native trees on a steep hillside above the sea.

Having become re-accustomed to these attractive surroundings, another quite different one lies in wait. The sea constantly frets even the hardest rocks of this coast and periodic undermining causes landslips on the slopes above. Here also the path has been carried away and further progress requires a climb through trees and steep Wheatham Combe. The effort is further increased if misleading cattle tracks in this combe lead to futile detours.

On arriving at the sloping fields above, the route turns east along a track. Later there are enclosing hedges and, in the vicinity of Broomstreet Farm, even a short stretch of tarmac. The house and outbuildings appear to be nineteenth century but could have replaced earlier ones on the same site. From here there is an enclosed peaceful track for the $1\frac{1}{2}$ miles to Silcombe Farm.

Compensation for the slow climb up Wheatham Combe comes in the form of a smooth almost level walking surface which encourages a fast easy walking pace. The track passes along a narrow shelf of sloping farmland sandwiched between the steep tree covered hillside falling directly into the sea and a higher harsher terrain of rough grazing, moorland and tree plantations. Only local farmers and walkers from afar now use this way. It epitomises peace and quiet, but might have been busier before the main coast road higher up the hill came into use.

At Silcombe the Coast Path turns left along the edge of a meadow and then passes through trees towards Culbone. It was not far from here, probably at Ash Farm, that Coleridge penned the lines of his famous incomplete poem 'Kubla Khan', in between waking from a feverish drugged sleep and being disturbed by an unknown unwelcome visitor from Porlock.

Near the start of the descent bushes and trees frame a picture postcard view of Hurlstone Point across Porlock Bay. The Point may still be distant but is now much closer than before. Then, enveloped by dense old oak woodland, the track leads down to the brink of the steep slope above the sea and the sound of the waves before turning inland and down towards Culbone on the valley floor.

Culbone is the second small coastal valley on this stretch where man has found a permanent home. The settlement is situated in a narrow north facing valley covered in trees. Its origins are in the Dark Ages and possibly before. No roads come to this place of peace and quiet which is nowadays reduced to a tiny church and two homes.

The past was different because this was once a charcoal burning centre. For centuries iron making was carried out at many small local sites using charcoal as fuel. Then during the early years of the Industrial Revolution coke made from coal was found to be just as effective and a great deal cheaper. With this innovation, charcoal burning declined and iron making became concentrated in parts of Wales, the Midlands and the North.

Culbone

Previously Culbone would have been busy and smoky, the complete antithesis of the quiet, enclosed and rather mysterious little place which visitors find today. By tradition charcoal burners were lepers, an isolated occupation which suited their banishment from society. It was said that the afflicted workers hereabouts were once more numerous than the deer in the surrounding woods. Culbone's little place of worship is a gem, the smallest complete parish church in the country and said to be capable of seating 33 people at a pinch. The building is simple with a lofty nave reminiscent of those found in surviving Anglo-Saxon churches. Parts of the building could date from those times but the structure is basically twelfth century. The eye-catching little spire may have been added as late as the nineteenth century. The name 'Culbone' derives from the Celtic 'Kil Beun', meaning 'the church of Bueno'. He lived in the sixth century and was yet another of the many Celtic saints who have left their mark in the West Country. Culbone is now a tourist attraction and it is rare to find solitude here but such is its spell that all who come respect and become part of its tranquillity.

The former coast path from Culbone to Porlock Weir was lost in a landslip and its replacement follows a higher route. The sound of the waves, muted during the stay in the hamlet, returns and remains in the background all the way to Porlock Weir. Even along the new path signs of slippage are everywhere

Porlock Weir

in uprooted trees, basins in the ground and abrupt changes of level. The approximate age of these slips may be judged from the size of the bushes and trees which have recolonised them. Ultimately the new route will follow the old down into the sea.

The first sign of Porlock Weir comes in the form of decorative pines, followed by a view of Hurlstone Point across nearby Porlock Bay. The path then becomes sunken and passes under an arch followed by a short tunnel. These features were both decorations and a means of hiding tradesmen from view as they made their way to the kitchens of Ashley Combe Lodge. The Lodge was a large Victorian Italianate house which was demolished in the 1940s after many years of neglect. Few traces now remain.

A new scene of meadows and a shingle shore comes into view ahead. At Worthy the way passes an attractive gatehouse built in the style of old local thatched cottages. Once part of the Ashley Combe Estate it is now a toll house on the road from Porlock Weir to the main coastal highway at Culbone Stables. The final stretch to Porlock Weir lies over these meadows with the shingle bank, creek, buildings and boats in full view ahead.

Porlock acquired its name when the local port became silted, or 'locked', in the Middle Ages. As roads were poor a replacement was essential and the obvious choice was Porlock Weir where a natural creek had formed behind an impressive shingle bank. This provided a safe haven for the small sailing vessels which carried goods to and from the Vale of Porlock. During the nineteenth century lock gates were added to accommodate larger ships. Cargoes included exports of farm products, timber and bark and imports of limestone for soil sweetening and coal. For a time wooden ships were also built beside the quay.

This trade died out in the early years of the twentieth century after the roads serving the area had begun to improve, the railway had arrived a few miles away and when the new much larger screw-driven steel ships were confined to larger ports. Nowadays leisure activities have transformed the little port and the car park by the shore has become the new focus of activity. Yet when there are no crowds this is still a rewarding place to dally, slowly taking in the little harbour with its gleaming vessels and then looking beyond at the massive sky, the wide sea and the curving bay leading up to the rocks of Hurlstone Point.

A legendary event involving Lynmouth, Porlock Weir and the road between was re-enacted on 12 January 1999, exactly one hundred years later. On that day in 1899 a large vessel, the *Forest Hall* of Liverpool, was caught in a severe gale off Porlock Weir. Its rudder had been carried away and both anchors were dragging. An urgent telegram requesting the Lynmouth lifeboat's help was sent from Porlock Weir but launching conditions there were too bad. However the volunteer crew, unwilling to abandon those on board, hauled their rowing

Wash day at Porlock Weir

lifeboat, the *Louisa*, for fourteen miles over high moors to the more sheltered Porlock Weir. The crew, helpers and cart horses tramped through a long wild wet winter night over the then narrow, twisting and rough road. Although physically drained, on arrival at the Weir they still managed to row out to the stricken vessel, help the crew haul up their anchors after a tug had arrived and then accompany it across to Barry in South Wales.

This herculean effort to save the lives of strangers fully deserved commemoration a hundred years later. A willing suitably dressed crew, stout horses, and a lifeboat of similar design to the *Louisa* took part but on this occasion they were followed for at least part of the way by walkers and vehicles. As before the sky was cloudy and the rain descended but there was no wind.

Porlock Bay

The third detour from the South West Coast Path starts nearby and leads to a very recent feature. Until 1996 there was a large continuous shingle bank all the way across Porlock Bay. This natural feature protected the low lying coastal meadows and also provided a very attractive route for the Coast Path.

Several local beaches, including Glenthorne, are also formed from these rounded stones. Most have their origins in rocks shattered during the Ice Ages and under the combined action of tides, storms and currents many have moved eastwards into Porlock Bay. For some time it had been evident that the movement of stones to the western end of the shingle bank had declined and that this section was becoming weak. Then on a very wild night in October 1996, the bank was overtopped by the sea in several places and at the worst spot, about half a mile to the east of Porlock Weir, a major breach was created.

Since then tides have flowed in and out of this gap. The former fresh water marsh behind the bank rapidly became a sea marsh and the outward flow on each ebb tide has created an impressive waterfall and tail race which erodes the underlying clay and is gradually extending inland. Thus former stability has been replaced by constant change and there is much speculation about where it all might end. At the extreme Porlock could recover its lost medieval harbour.

If time is available and the tide conditions are right for the white water display, usually about two hours after high water, it is worthwhile strolling up to the breach from Porlock Weir, first along the shore and then along the shingle bank. No attempt should be made to cross the breach at any stage of the tide.

For those who might wish to walk no further at this time there is a bus service from Porlock Weir to Porlock and Minehead. From Porlockford a bridleway, later becoming a path, leads to Porlock village along the bottom of a steep wooded hillside. Gaps in foliage on the left provide glimpses of the bay, the breach, the new salt water lagoon, Hurlstone Point and the gardens of several nearby houses. To the right there are only trees, climbing up and away out of sight. They form part of the great natural forest which, with very few breaks extends from the valleys of Horner and East Waters to the steep coastal slopes near the Foreland.

Sessile oaks were valuable to man and often encouraged to grow at the expense of other species. Repeated coppicing of these trees has often led to weird shapes which at times of poor light appear threatening or even spectral. The timber had numerous uses but the bark's was unique. It provided tannin for leather making. This was exported and also used in the large tannery at Porlock which remained in operation until relatively recent times. The buildings still survive but now have miscellaneous uses.

Set in a fertile vale, with high beautiful hills on three sides and the sea on the fourth, Porlock would appear especially favoured. But like most local places it has had its ups and downs. It lost its original port, has seen the once plentiful fisheries dwindle and die, watched helplessly as the prosperous wool trade moved away to the north and observed the tanning industry come and go.

Nowadays tourism is the economic pillar but the village has also become a popular residential centre. Only a few of the original stone and thatched buildings remain but their replacements, some getting on in years themselves, appear to have the same random positioning as before. While this was of little consequence in the old packhorse and horse and cart days, nowadays when road traffic is heavy, parking rife and two large commercial vehicles or tourist coaches meet at a narrow corner in the main street, the outcome can be bedlam.

The church tower is the prime architectural feature. The truncated spire lost its top in a storm centuries ago. Below this the massive stonework with few openings, seems to be more of a place of refuge than an edifice built to the glory

Porlock Church Tower

of God and it may well have served both purposes. The patron saint is Saint Dubricius, a name with unfortunate connotations of dubious, duplicitous and suspicious. He was yet another of the many Celtic saints who brought Christianity to these parts. Dubricius also has a very special claim to fame as the priest who solemnised the marriage between King Arthur and Guinevere.

Porlock has a number of shops, eating places and accommodation ranging from hotels to a camp site. The village is also on several bus routes.

⇥ STAGE 10 ⇤

PORLOCK TO MINEHEAD

The final stage takes the walker back to Minehead. On the way the Vale of Porlock is left behind for a high wild coast where Exmoor's eastern hills meet the sea.

From Porlock Church the walk follows Villes Lane towards the sea for a quarter of a mile and at its end a hedge-enclosed footpath heads away across fields. Roads and dwellings are now replaced by arable land. The last encounter with similar farm country was near Washford 80 miles back along the way. The present near-level fields are said to be revered by beer drinkers for the quality of their malting barley but in recent times the crop beside the way has more often than not been wheat.

After several direction changes, the narrow enclosed track briefly becomes a field edge path with wider views. The damaged shingle bank and low horizon on the left hint at the sea's presence and the village of Bossington lies ahead. But neither of these capture the eye: that is the prerogative of beautiful massive Bossington Hill, covered in grass, bracken and heather. Its dominance increases with each step forward, constantly reminding the walker that the approaching climb will go even higher. This hill stands at the western end of an extensive moorland ridge which confronts the sea along the whole of its length. Hedges return to bound the way and, after a detour around an old farm, the route enters Bossington's main street. This is an attractive National Trust village formerly owned by the Acland family and the old thatched and tiled cottages and houses have been carefully preserved. The massive stone chimneys projecting onto the street attract special attention. Many of the properties are very old, built before chimneys were commonplace, and one hates to think of living conditions at the time. Open fires, used for both cooking and heating, were located in central positions within the structures and the smoke, drifting slowly upwards, contaminated both humans and their possessions before percolating through the thatch to the open air above. It is said that when chimneys first arrived, the more well-to-do members of the community who were able to afford this innovation had them erected in these prominent positions to serve as constant reminders to their less fortunate neighbours.

One corner of Bossington has a tortuous connection through distant places with a site encountered earlier. One of the village dwellings is known as Banksia House. This name comes from a genus of shrubs named after Sir Joseph Banks, a wealthy man and friend of Captain Cook who accompanied the

Bossington

explorer on one of his South Sea voyages as the expedition's official botanist. The original seeds which produced today's Banksia presumably came back with him from Australasia.

The Banks' family home was at Revesby Abbey in Lincolnshire, a large residence built on the site of the former Abbot's House. Before dissolution Revesby had been a Cistercian monastery and it was from here in the twelfth century that monks and the newly promoted abbot travelled across the country to found Cleeve Abbey.

Nowadays Banks is best remembered in his native Lincolnshire and at Kew Gardens where he was the first director. However when he and Cook returned home in 1771 with 1300 dried specimens of new species from the other side of the world and the surviving half of *Endeavour's* ship's company it was Banks and not Cook who received the hero's welcome. The reason is not hard to find. Banks was a member of the revered and sometimes feared ruling class of the country and Cook was only a commoner.

The route turns left at a cottage with a Swiss-style wooden balcony on its gable end. This resembles the similar feature at Cloutsham farm, seen earlier from the flanks of Dunkery Beacon. As both properties are part of the Holnicote Estate it is very likely that the same Acland family members were responsible for both. The River Aller and Horner Water join at the outskirts of Bossington. The combined stream then passes between the village and the lower slopes of Bossington Hill to enter marshland before seeping through the shingle bank to the sea. The walk leaves the village near the car park, crosses a footbridge over the river and then follows a well used track through trees.

The long climb to the tops begins gently. Glimpses through the foliage on the left reveal meadows, the shingle bank and the sea. But on the right there is only the towering bulk of Bossington Hill. Then the surroundings become more open and the old look out station and the crags of Hurlstone Point come into view ahead. From here a long slog leads up steep high Hurlstone Combe. During the climb gorse, small trees and lush bracken give way to bare scree overlooked by short heather. This is a harsh place when winter gales funnel in off the sea but in late summer it makes a beautiful picture with the light grey of a multitude of scattered rocks providing a perfect contrast for the dazzling purple of heather.

At the top, the walk leaves the South West Coast Path, having followed it for more than 20 miles. The new path, known as the 'Rugged Coast Path', is joined some distance ahead. This name is a misnomer because its surface and immediate surroundings are no more than rough. However there is a long section where the ground drops away for 650 feet into the sea, making conditions potentially dangerous if the weather is wild. In these circumstances the South West Coast Path provides a suitable alternative for although it passes over exposed moorland there are no steep slopes.

During this long walk several different types of tracks and paths have been followed, including permissive routes across Crown Land or land owned by the National Park and National Trust. The Rugged Coast Path is a permissive path across land owned by the last and is exceptional in that the permission does not extend to dogs.

A rest at the top of Hurlstone Combe provides an opportunity to enjoy the wider view. The long line of hogs-back hills extending away to the Foreland holds the eye not only for its beauty but because it encompasses almost all the previous stage.

The Rugged Coast Path is reached along the top of the high coast towards East Combe. Here a large mass of ground has slumped towards the shore and halted on the way down, leaving a large grass-covered shelf between the top and the water. Below restless currents swirl off Hurlstone Point at all stages of the tide with nearby Selworthy Sands, exposed at low water, mirroring this turbulence with deep flow patterns across their surface.

Ahead lies East Combe, its bleak seaward scree-covered entrance only softened once a year when heather blooms. The former tree-covered hillsides above the sea between the Foreland and Porlock Weir are now no more. This latest part of the Exmoor coast, with its harsh empty slopes tumbling into the

Above East Combe looking west to the Atlantic

water, resembles the far west beyond Woody Bay. Although East Combe is small its upper reaches have a much softer face with a covering of grass and bracken. The size of this valley and the heights of the prominent surrounding hills are deceptive because there is nothing to provide a measure for the eye and it is easy to imagine being amongst higher wider hills further north.

The path heads into the upper reaches of East Combe, where the rounded hillocks at its head mark the start of the Rugged Coast Path. In recent years this path has become popular but winter walks are often solitary affairs and then all thoughts of living on a crowded island can easily be brushed aside.

Breasting the rise on East Combe's eastern side, the walk rounds a corner and heads into Henners Combe. This is deeper, longer and less harsh than its predecessor. As before the path turns inland, descends to cross two small streams in the bottom and then climbs up the opposite bank, heading back towards the sea.

Some inconspicuous lumps of concrete and pieces of rusty iron are visible in this valley. These date from World War Two when the ridge was used as a battle training ground for American and Canadian Forces preparing for D-Day and the subsequent reconquest of Continental Europe. The meadows on the high ground to the east of the valley also reveal some nondescript features partly obscured by undergrowth. Although now difficult imagine, these were part of a tank firing range. A target trolley hauled by cable once passed to and fro across this hillside as a succession of tanks, lumbering around the moorland summit of nearby Selworthy Beacon, fired at it in turn.

When I first walked along this moorland ridge in 1951, the ground surface was still badly torn by tank tracks and I wondered whether it would ever recover. However I misjudged the combined healing effects of nature and time. Although ammunition and other mementoes may still lurk below, the surface has recovered and reveals few traces of its turbulent past.

At the seaward end of the eastern flank of Henners Combe, the path makes another abrupt turn and passes onto the top of a steep slope 650 feet above the sea. This extends eastwards for one and a half miles. Ahead and uphill a few dead and dying pines stand out against the sky. I have been told that their present and past sufferings are not due the harsh surroundings but to lead poisoning from machine gun bullets fired into them long ago.

One short section of the path is always wet and muddy regardless of the season. The source of the water is a spring higher up the hill which once met the needs of the people and animals at nearby West Myne Farm. For centuries this settlement stood in an exposed but beautiful position where the gently undulating tops begin to fall away with increasing speed towards the sea. It would have been a terrible place when cold winter gales came roaring in from the Atlantic, not only due to exposure and discomfort but also the lonely isolation which came with them. Yet on lovely summer days the farm's surroundings would have been beautiful, especially when the dominating blues of the sea and the sky gradually changed to gold with the coming of night.

During World War Two the farm's inhabitants and their stock were moved to make way for the wartime battle training area. Surviving photographs show a substantial and attractive old house set in a slight dip in the hillside. There is now only a minimal ruin on the site. It is on private land and not open to the public. The buildings were destroyed during the war and nobody came back.

However the fields are still worked from Hindon and Wydon Farms, 2 miles away below the south facing slopes of the ridge, so cattle and sheep are now the only residents of these uplands. Although only 4 miles from Minehead, West Myne was remote because there was only a rough stony track connecting the farm to the town. It is one of life's ironies that the popular road which now runs along the length of the ridge only came with the war which destroyed the house and farm buildings. The former inhabitants would have had to have been self sufficient and no doubt grew much of their own food. There is a story, one hopes apocryphal, of a girl arriving at the farm as the farmer's new wife and only leaving it again in her coffin after mothering sixteen children. Whether true or not it provides an insight to the harsh life once lived up here.

Although the path is safe in calm weather, the distant sound of waves breaking on the shore far below sometimes wings up through the void to provide a sharp reminder of the true nature of the terrain. One part of the hillside has vestiges of former trees and in spring the ground is still covered with dwarf bluebells which can cope with the exposed environment. On special sunny days the deep blue of this carpet vies with those of the sea below and the sky above.

Later in the year, after the flowering heather is past its best and the bracken has turned brown, small isolated rowans redress the balance of nature's fading colours with masses of orange-red berries. The coast eventually veers to the right, revealing a glimpse of the meadows and shingle shore far below at Greenaleigh. Near the path old landslides have left rough rocky hillocks across the face of the steep slope now recolonised by vegetation. This is a wildlife haven, confirmed by sparrow hawks above, riding the steady updraft in their near effortless hovering hunting. Known as the Brockholes, this place was probably named after the badgers who made it their home.

At length the path reaches a prominent high point above the entrance to Grexy Combe. Here the walk turns away from the sea into this valley which is the largest of the three encountered along this stretch of the coast. As before raw scree hangs above the seaward entrance but inland the wild vegetation becomes lush. Each spring a jungle of flowering gorse covers the hillsides with masses of dazzling yellow and in early summer the bottom becomes a carpet of flowering orchids. As in Henners Combe, the path crosses two small streams in the bottom but then climbs back to the top through a side valley.

The Rugged Coast Path ends at the top. Beyond the boundary fence and stile the way is eastwards aross the open moor, ignoring paths to both right and left. After passing through the boundary banks of long abandoned fields it then joins the South West Coast Path. The old fields once belonged to one of several farms up here. Long ago the ground would have been recovered from the moor with anticipation and energy but in the end the farmers were obliged to retreat and the wild has returned.

A small group of weather beaten trees and bushes is visible on the top of the ridge ahead. At a distance these give no hint of being the edge of extensive

Brockholes, Rugged Coast Path

woods which cover the sides and top of the hill as it approaches Minehead. A backward glance over Grexy Combe and the recently traversed path reveals a feature on top of Fursebury Brake which was not visible before. This is a modest circular Iron Age ditch and bank. Given the location and the nature of the surrounding terrain it would have been constructed to protect the folk of West Myne and other former farms in the vicinity. From this observation one could conclude that although the last inhabitants may only left this ridge relatively recently, before this it provided homes and sustenance for many generations over thousands of years.

Beside a simple seat at the next path junction, the Coast Path leaves the top of the broad ridge and heads down the slope towards the sea. Then at the point where the gradient becomes steep, it turns eastwards to make a slow descent along the face of this coastal hill.

Another path heads straight down the very steep slope into Burgundy Combe on a more roundabout route to Minehead. This is the last of the many little valleys opening to the sea along the way from Heddon's Mouth, now some 30 miles to the rear. The remnants of tiny Burgundy Chapel stand near the bottom beside a minuscule stream. It is believed to have been built by a member of the Luttrell family, the major local landowners for hundreds of years, possibly to celebrate his safe return from the Burgundian Wars. These were fought at a time when the Norman overlords of this country still laid claim to much of France.

During the gradual descent along the Coast Path, which hereabouts is both well made and well trodden, the surroundings, beginning with moorland and wide views over the sea, change to nearby bushes, then small trees and finally to a high thick canopy. The last can shade the sun, moderate the wind, or provide shelter from the rain. The vehicle track from Greenaleigh climbs to join the route which then acquires a tarmac surface at the Exmoor National Park boundary. As the lane curves round the hill a large 'tent' comes into view directly ahead. The eye takes some time to escape from this to the restrained and much more attractive wider scene. Now the familiar rugged Exmoor coast has gone, replaced by a low lying shore backed by marshland leading up to wooded hills and a distant backdrop of the lovely rolling Quantocks. Seaside scenes change with weather, time of day and season but Minehead Bay is also subject to the Bristol Channel's wide ranging tides so the middle distance alternates rapidly between a wide plain of sand and mud and a sea seemingly about to engulf the adjacent low lying land.

The junction with Beacon Road marks the beginning of suburban Minehead. Here the walk does not follow the South West Coast Path down the zig zag path towards the harbour but continues along Burgundy Road into Martlet Road, another leafy highway. It descends to the town centre where this walk around

Exmoor began and now ends. However rewarding a long walk might be, there are always moments, especially if blisters are complaining, when the end is anticipated with joy. Yet when the moment comes, there is no elation or even modest pleasure, just a feeling of deflation. Mirroring life, it is not the end which matters but the journey itself.

Back at Minehead

ADVICE FOR WALKERS

So far the book has described the pleasures and points of interest along my route around Exmoor. The present section now gives practical advice for those who might wish to go out and discover it for themselves.

DISCLAIMER

While every effort has been made to ensure the accuracy of the advice given, the author cannot be held responsible for any mishaps which might befall walkers along the way.

A WEATHER WARNING

Although Exmoor may have a kinder climate than the high hills in other parts of Britain, its weather should never be taken for granted.
Two considerations are very important-
(1) Wind, rain, snow and cold are always more severe on the open tops than in the nearby valley bottoms.
(2) Weather conditions can change rapidly and may have serious consequences if they worsen.

The sharp contrast between the sparse vegetation of the moorland tops and the lush growth of delicate plants in the valley bottoms provides a constant reminder of two very different but adjacent climates.

With the foregoing in mind certain basic precautions should always be taken before going out onto Exmoor's lonely moors or high coast.

(1) Check the weather forecast beforehand and, if necessary, modify the route to suit. If the way is exposed and the weather likely to deteriorate it is wise to consider both alternative and escape routes.
(2) Always wear good walking boots and carry both rain gear and some extra warm clothing.
(3) Carry a compass and an adequate map, having first gained competence in using them together.
(4) Carry a first aid kit at all times and a torch on short winter days.
(5) Carry sufficient drink and food to meet all anticipated needs.
(6) If the walk is a lone one always leave details of the proposed route behind with a responsible person.

Stages (4), (7), (9) Part 1 and (10) have the greatest potential for exposure but this does not imply that conditions cannot be adverse elsewhere.

MAPS FOR WAYFINDING

The map in this book is for orientation purposes only. By far the best wayfinding map is the O.S. Outdoor Leisure Map No.9, Exmoor. It is in the large 1:25000 scale and depicts all field boundaries. This map also covers the whole of the route.

During preparations for the walk it is suggested that the route might be marked lightly in pencil on a copy of this map using the detailed information and grid references given later in this section.

For those who are not yet familiar with grid references, all Ordnance Survey maps have a numbered grid superimposed on them. The first three numbers of a six numbered grid reference are eastings, i.e. from left to right across the map, and the second three are northings i.e. from bottom to top up the map. By using the two sets of three numbers it is then possible to pinpoint any spot on the map.

THE STARTING POINT FOR THE WALK

As the route is circular the beginning can be anywhere along it. However there are good reasons for starting and finishing at Minehead.

(1) It is a convenient access point from the rest of the country.
(2) As Exmoor's main population centre it has the widest choice of accommodation, shops and all other facilities.
(3) It is the main focal point for public transport around Exmoor.

SUMMARY OF THE ROUTE (Excluding Recommended Short Detours)

STAGE	START AND FINISH	DISTANCE		APPROXIMATE TIME REQUIRED
		Miles	Kilometres	Hours
1	Minehead to Watchet	7.5	12	4.5
2	Watchet to Dunster	11.0	18	7.0
3	Dunster to Horner	7.0	11	4.5
4	Horner to Exford	8.0	13	5.0
5	Exford to Withypool	13.0	21	8.5
6	Withypool to Simonsbath	6.0	10	3.5
7	Simonsbath to Lynton	10.0	16	6.5
8	Lynton round to Lynmouth	12.0	19	8.0
9	Lynmouth to Porlock			
	Part One	6.0	10	5.0
	Part Two	8.0	13	6.0
10	Porlock to Minehead	8.0	13	6.0
	TOTAL	**96.5**	**156**	

Please Note-

(1) The distances quoted above do not include the recommended detours which can add 2-3 miles to a day's walk.

(2) The timings are only approximate as each walker has an individual pace. Allowances have been made for sightseeing and the type of terrain but not for meal stops or the recommended detours.

(3) If Stage (9) is not split into two as suggested, the total walking time will be approximately nine hours.

ACCOMMODATION ARRANGEMENTS AND LOCAL TRANSPORT

There are two basic accommodation choices. Walkers can either use overnight stops at the end of each stage or as far as possible make use of public transport to get to and from accommodation bases in Minehead and Lynmouth/Lynton. One advantage of the latter is that the load carried on most days is much reduced. Arrangements will suit individual requirements but one accommodation example, based on current summer bus timetables, is as follows.

(1) Take a bus back to Minehead from Watchet at the end of Stage (1) and return the following morning.

(2) At the end of Stage (2) there are buses between Minehead and Dunster.

(3) There are buses between Minehead and a point near Horner at the end of Stage (3).

(4) At the end of Stage (4) there are buses beteeen Exford and Minehead.

(5) At the end of Stage (5) taxis could be used between Withypool and Lynton/Lynmouth.

(6) At the end of Stage (6) taxis could be used between Simonsbath and Lynton/Lynmouth.

(7) & (8) Stage (7) ends at Lynmouth/Lynton and Stage (8) also begins and ends at Lynton/Lynmouth.

(9) Stage (9) ends at Porlock and there are buses between this village and Minehead.

(10) A further night might be spent at Minehead at the end of Stage (10).

Summarising the above, nights 1-5 inclusive could be spent at Minehead (assuming an overnight stop there before starting out), nights 6-8 at Lynton/Lynmouth and nights 9-10 back at Minehead again.

Please Note-
That the above example is based CURRENT 2000 summer bus services. There is no guarantee that these will remain unchanged in future.

One further accommodatiom pattern might appeal to walkers wishing to take a more leisurely walk around the route spread over two holidays, one at Minehead and the other at Lynton /Lynmouth. The walk from Minehead to Exford and back from Porlock to Minehead could be made from Minehead and the remainder from a second holiday base at Lynton/Lynmouth.

INFORMATION ON PUBLIC TRANSPORT

A comprehensive summer public transport guide for Exmoor and West Somerset, covering the period from the beginning of June to the end of September, is published each year. There is also a similar more restricted winter timetable. These can be obtained free of charge from all local tourist and Exmoor National Park visitor centres. In addition Watchet and Minehead are connected by train services for most of the year. It should be noted that two very useful bus services. No. 285 'The North Exmoor Visitor Bus', and the No.300 Minehead/Lynton only run regularly between the beginning of June and the end of September. The following summary lists the most useful but not necessarily exclusive bus services from and to the walk route-

Watchet to Minehead and return - Service No. 28

Dunster to Minehead and return - Service No. 34
Porlock to Minehead and return - Services No. 38 and No. 300
Exford to Minehead and return - Service No. 285
County Gate to Minehead or Lynmouth - Service No. 300
Unfortunately the former 'Heart of Exmoor Link' Service No. 295, connecting Withypool, Simonsbath and Lynton, has now been withdrawn.

ACCOMMODATION

Exmoor has a wide choice of accommodation at the larger population centres of Minehead and Lynmouth/Lynton. Elsewhere it is more limited. Booking ahead is strongly recommended, especially during the holiday season. Up to date detailed information on accommodation can be obtained from the local tourist information centres.

POSSIBLE ROUTE MODIFICATIONS

SOME LESS DEMANDING ALTERNATIVES

The walk is intended as an easy-paced if somewhat lengthy sightseeing perambulation. However some walkers might wish to make changes to suit personal requirements. For their benefit the following are suggested.

Stages (5), (8) and (9) are rather long but can be shortened or changed.
Stage (5) can be reduced slightly by eliminating the detour down to Tarr Steps. The modified route will then head upstream rather than downstream on first reaching the River Barle (GR 861326). An alternative method of reducing Stage (5) would be an overnight stop in the vicinity of Tarr Steps rather than at Withypool or Lynton/Lynmouth.
Accommodation is available in the Tarr steps area. This change would of course lengthen Stage (6) which was a planned easy rest day in the middle of the walk. Stage (8) can be shortened on reaching Slattenslade near Woody Bay (GR 678483) by heading straight down the hill to join the South West Coast Path as it follows the lane towards Lynton.
In many respects it would be a pity to miss Tarr Steps (Stage (5)) and the Heddon Valley with its very beautiful stretch of the coast (Stage (8)). Another alternative would be to complete Stage (8) over two days using a taxi to and from Woody Bay. Stage (9) can be split into two with a break at County Gate. In addition to reducing the day's walk length it also allows walkers to take full advantage of the many points of interest and recommended detours along the way. The description of Stage (9) which follows sets out both the single and split stage

alternatives. At present the No. 300 bus service only runs regularly past County Gate during the summer months.

SOME MORE CHALLENGING ALTERNATIVES

Although not intended to be a challenge, some might prefer a long fast walk. They could consider combining Stages 3 & 4 (15 miles). Stages 6 & 7 (16 miles) and not splitting up Stage 9 (14 miles).

If walkers embark on an unhurried walk it will take them 10 or 12 days. The faster version outlined immediately above, requires 8. Those who have only a week or less available can take some recommended short cuts which are set out in the SHORT CUT section following the DETAILED NOTES. Basically these leave out Watchet by proceeding directly from Dunster Beach to Dunster and eliminate Stage (8) from Lynton to the Heddon Valley and back. This arrangement removes the peripheral parts of the walk but leaves the central section unchanged.

DETAILED WAYFINDING NOTES FOR EACH STAGE

STAGE (1) MINEHEAD to WATCHET, 7.5 Miles (12 Kilometres).

(1)   Minehead beach is partly obstructed by new groynes and except at low tide the best way forward is eastwards along the promenade.

(2)   The beach and shingle bank to the east of the promenade are reached by a footpath which begins along the side of the golf club house (GR 984464).

(3)   A public footpath follows the top of the sea bank from Minehead to Blue Anchor but if the tide is out the beach is more pleasurable and often provides a better walking surface.

(4)   During the summer months there are toilets and a small open air café at Dunster Beach car park (GR 004445).

(5)   In addition to the railway station (services to Minehead and Watchet), Blue Anchor has several cafés, most only open during the summer months, and a pub/hotel at its eastern end. There are also public toilets half way along the promenade (GR 027434).

(6)   The shore walk from Blue Anchor to Watchet should not be attempted when the tide is flooding as there is a danger of becoming trapped below the cliffs. Tide times should be checked beforehand.

(7)   Due to cliff falls the alternative cliff top walk no longer starts along the edge of the small meadow immediately to the east of the inn. In order to reach the remaining part of the cliff path it is now necessary to follow the coast road up the hill for half a mile before turning left through trees. This turning point is opposite a caravan park entrance on the right (GR 039432). Care is needed along the narrow often busy road.

(8) At Warren Bay (GR 055433) there is access from the cliff down to the alternative shore route and vice versa.

(9) From Daws Castle (GR 062433) the cliff top route follows either the coast road down into Watchet or, preferably, the footpath leading down to Whitehall (GR 062431), a relatively quiet road leading to the centre of the little town.

(10) Watchet has a full range of facilities, including shops, cafés, restaurants and accommodation. Bus Services Nos. 15, 28 and 300 provide connections back to Minehead. The bus stop is at the top of Swain Street, adjacent to the footbridge over the railway. Alternatively trains, some hauled by steam, also go to Minehead for most of the year.

STAGE (2) WATCHET to DUNSTER, 11 Miles (18 Kilometres).

(1) The walk starts by heading inland along Swain Street, Watchet's main thoroughfare. After crossing the road bridge over the railway it turns onto a tarmac footpath on its immediate right. This heads away from the road and up the hill to St Decuman's Church.

(2) In front of the church the route turns right onto a track leading downhill. This becomes a footpath over fields to Kentsford Farm (GR 058425).

(3) After passing through the farmyard and crossing the small stream, a track leads up to the former mineral railway, now a path. Here the route turns left.

(4) On reaching Washford along the old mineral line, the path crosses a recreation ground and enters a lane in front of the village school. Here the route turns right. At a road tee junction with a railway bridge on the right it heads straight across to join a footpath passing gardens of dwellings on the left and the railway embankment on the right.

(5) At the railway station the route turns left along the main road for a short distance. Immediately beyond the filling station on the right there is a footpath on the right (GR 045410). This heads south, climbing steadily along field edges and later becomes a track. If a detour to Cleeve Abbey (GR 047406) is planned, this is reached by continuing along the main road past the filling station and then taking the first right turn signposted to Roadwater. This detour is half a mile long.

(6) On emerging onto a road junction (GR 036396) the route joins a tarmac lane continuing in the same westerly direction. This lane marks the boundary of Exmoor National Park.

(7) On reaching Felon's Oak (GR 018388), the lane again becomes a track which climbs more steeply, crosses Stout's Way Lane and 1.5 miles beyond

Felon's Oak reaches the conifer plantation above Monkslade Common close to the top of Monkham Hill (GR 994389).

(8) The route continues on as a forest track to a track junction above Perley Combe (GR 983393) where it turns right, north and downhill for approximately three quarters of a mile.

(9) On descending to another track junction (GR 987406), a left turn leads westwards and down into Long Combe. At the combe bottom the route turns right and downhill beside the stream.

(10) The stream is followed out of the valley to another track junction (GR 988414) where a track commences to climb eastwards. The route now has helpful pairs of Crown Estate walk markers which also point the way at two further turns. Bat's Castle stands at the top (GR 988421).

(11) From Bat's Castle the path continues over Gallox Hill and then drops into trees. Here the route turns right (GR 983428), abandoning the Crown Estate walk markers which point to the left.

(12) The path continues to descend, eventually joining a well used track approaching from the left. This leads to Gallox Bridge on the outskirts of Dunster (GR 989431).

(13) Dunster has a few shops, a number of restaurants, a range of accommodation and a plethora of tea places. Minehead is only 2 miles away and bus services Nos. 34 and 290 connect the two places. The bus stops are at the Foresters Arms, the terminus of the No. 34 bus service, and in the market place.

STAGE (3) DUNSTER to HORNER, 7 Miles (11 Kilometres).

(1) From Dunster Market Place the walk heads northwards away from the castle and up the Ball and then turns left into Priory Green. This lane, behind the backs of the Market Place properties, is followed through the old priory and past the tithe barn up to the primary school ahead. To the right of this school a tarmac track heads uphill past an old cemetery and later turns left past allotments on the right. Continuing as a path heading uphill through trees, the route turns right at a path tee junction (GR 987434) and up to a track where a left turn (GR 982438) leads up to the top of Grabbist Hill.

(2) The way forward is now westwards, following an obvious track along the top of the ridge for the next 2 miles. After three quarters of a mile the surrounding open moorland is replaced by forestry plantations.

(3) Immediately ahead of the trig. point marked on the map as a 295 metres spot height (GR 948442), the route takes a left turn and descends to the south-west along a forest track. This narrows to a path (GR 943437) and then descends through old enclosures, now heavily wooded. Eventually a stile leads to a meadow which descends to a highway. From here the route is to the right along Wootton Courtenay's main street (GR 938433).

(4) At a crossroads (GR 935434) the route turns left along the dead end lane terminating at Brockwell (GR 928431).

(5) From Brockwell and the route follows the near level track on the right heading north west. This is initially hedge enclosed. It passes along the foot of the Dunkery Range and is followed for 1.5 miles to to a point close to Luccombe (GR 908442). Here a right turn into the lane known as Stoney Street leads to the village centre.

(6) A footpath from the churchyard close to Luccombe church tower is followed to the right and westwards (GR 910445). This leads to a lane and then up to the minimal remains of an old chapel close to Chapel Cross (GR 905448).

(7) After passing through a field gate on the opposite side of the road from the remains, the route turns right and follows a track to the north west along the boundary between the tree covered hillside on the left and farmland on the right. This track is followed to Horner.

(8) Horner has two tea gardens, open in season, public toilets and a car park. Porlock, over a mile away has shops, cafés, restaurants and accommodation. If there are no plans to visit Porlock at this stage, buses can be hailed three quarters of a mile to the north of Horner near the junction between the road from Horner and the A39 at Red Post (GR 897465). This junction is on an awkward bend so it is advisable to walk towards Porlock for a short distance where bus drivers can observe hand signals and stop.

STAGE (4) HORNER to EXFORD, 8 Miles (13 Kilometres).

(1) This stage commences by briefly retracing steps along Luccombe Lane to the track heading right and uphill from a point immediately beyond the converted water mill (GR 899453).

(2) After a short climb the route leaves the track and turns right along a path immediately behind the old water mill. This then follows the leat into Horner Valley. Neither the leat nor the path are depicted on the 0.S. Exmoor Map

(3) Some distance ahead there is a footbridge (GR 895445) over Horner Water, now on the immediate right. If the river is in spate a small section of the present path further upstream may be flooded and it is advisable to cross this bridge and turn left onto the main track up the valley. If this alternative is followed there is a branch track a quarter of a mile ahead on the left which heads into East Water (GR 896440).

(4) The path follows the water into East Water Valley and then joins the track up this valley. There are convenient footbridges at each ford along the way.

(5)   After half a mile, during which the valley becomes increasingly narrow, a narrow tarmac lane drops down to the stream and crosses it at a ford (GR 897430). Here the walk crosses the ford by the adjacent footbridge and heads eastwards up the lane for a short distance before turning right into steep Hollow Combe (GR 898430).

(6)   The route turns right at a path tee junction in Hollow Combe. There is a tendency to go uphill to the left but this is wrong. The correct right branch heads through trees and then out to the first path junction on the open hillside (GR 895428) where the way ahead is now to the left and uphill. At the second path junction on the open hillside (GR 895425) the way turns right, joining Dicky's Path. This descends slowly into Aller Combe (GR 893422) and then out on the other side to yet another junction close to the Sweetworthy Iron Age earthworks (GR 891424). Here the route heads left, south and steeply up to the summit of Dunkery Beacon. Over the next 4 miles the route is high and exposed. Aller Combe provides the only place of shelter along this part of the way.

(7)   From Dunkery Beacon the path to the west is followed to Rowbarrows (GR 875415). Here the route takes a dog leg turn onto another path, initially not very obvious, heading south-east to a track beside a beech boundary hedge (GR 880413). Here the route turns right and westwards.

(8)   This track is followed to the west for 1 mile where it joins a road (GR 860411) and veers left. On reaching the road junction at the 432 metres spot height (GR 854405), the route then turns left and south east into a hedge enclosed track.

(9)   After 250 yards there is right turn onto the bridleway heading south (GR 856404) which leads down to Exford. Although initially obscure, the bridleway soon becomes obvious, changing to a tarmac lane on the approach to the village.

(10) Exford has shops, pubs, accommodation and toilets. There is a useful bus service during the summer months, the No. 285, the 'North Exmoor Tourist Bus' to Porlock and Minehead. The bus stop is close to the small shelter at the corner of the village recreation ground.

STAGE (5) EXFORD to WITHYPOOL, 13 Miles (21 Kilometres).

This is one of the three physically challenging stages of the walk. If required it can be shortened somewhat by eliminating the visit to Tarr Steps or to a greater extent by staying overnight in the vicinity of this footbridge. Please refer to the earlier section on ALTERNATIVES.

(1)   This stage commences at the rather untidy entrance to the village car park. At the far end of the car park there is a footpath which heads south-east and downstream beside the river (GR 855382).

(2)   The path soon turns left away from the river, passing over a rise before rejoining the water again on the approach to the old farm at Lyncombe (GR 867375).

(3)   From Lyncombe a bridleway is followed above the river to Nethercote where the river is then crossed (GR 876361). From here another bridleway branches to the right and climbs the steep valley side to Bye Common (GR 887357) before dropping down to the Withypool-Winsford road (GR 892353). A standing stone and a signpost in the middle of a field provide a good waymark at GR 887357. During the south-easterly descent to the road this bridleway is not obvious but the field boundaries marked on the map give guidance on its whereabouts.

(4)   After turning right and westwards along the road for a quarter of a mile, a left turn along an access track leads south down to Withycombe Farm beside the Winn Brook (GR 887351). From the farm a bridleway heads up to and then along the right flank of the Punchbowl (GR 883349). Initially the route is not very obvious.

(5)   From the top of the Punchbowl, the Caratacus Stone (GR 889335) is reached by paths across the open moor or along the roadside verge.

(6)   On leaving the Caratacus Stone the walk follows the lane from Spire Cross heading south west to the edge of the moor (GR 884332) where it turns right onto a bridleway leading down to Knaplock (GR 869330) From here Watery Lane, another bridleway, is followed to the River Barle (GR 861326).

(7)   The east bank of the river is now followed downstream to Tarr Steps (GR 867321) which are crossed and the return upstream is made along the west bank footpath to a footbridge (GR 859327). This is used to cross back to the east bank.

(8)   The well marked and much used path along the east bank of the Barle is then followed upstream and northwards for the remaining 3 miles to Withypool.

(9)   Withypool is a small village with a pub, shop and some accommodation.

STAGE (6) WITHYPOOL to SIMONSBATH, 6 Miles (10 Kilometres).

This stage is short and intended to be a rest day in the middle of the walk. However if Stage (5) has been shortened because it is too demanding and the overnight stop is made in the vicinity of Tarr Steps then the length of the present stage will be increased to 10 miles.

(1)   Simonsbath is directly upstream from Withypool but the initial stages of the walk do not follow the Barle Valley. From the west side of Withypool's old village school, now an activity centre, a footpath crosses four small meadows in turn to reach tarmac covered Kitridge Lane (GR 841359), where the route turns left and north west.

(2)   Kitridge Lane climbs gently upwards for $1\frac{1}{2}$ miles until it becomes a track across open moorland in the vicinity of Landacre Lane (GR 824367) which is crossed. Then at the second of two track junctions on the open moor (GR 818370), the route veers left and south west, heading down to the River Barle in the valley bottom at Horsen Ford (GR 796369).

(3) At Horsen Ford the route does not cross the ford but continues along the river's north bank to Cow Castle (GR 793373).

(4) From Cow Castle there is a well trodden bridleway along the north side of the river to Simonsbath (GR 773392).

(5) Simonsbath is only a small village but it does have a café, a pub, accommodation and a car park with toilets.

STAGE (7) SIMONSBATH to LYNTON, 10 Miles (16 Kilometres).

Part of this stage is over the high moors at the source of the River Exe and can be exposed in bad weather.

(1) The starting point is the Exmoor National Park car park in the village of Simonsbath (GR 774394). Near the entry to the upper parking level a footpath heads off to the left.

(2) This path proceeds northwards through Ashcombe, passing through trees before climbing to the high pastures above the little valley. At the top of the hill (GR 775406) the route turns left and west along a rough pasture to the Simonsbath-Lynmouth road (GR 769407) where it turns right.

(3) A short distance along the road there is a layby on the left (GR 767410). A permissive bridleway starting from the layby but not shown on the map, leads westwards to Exe Head (GR 751415). On approaching Dure Down the route becomes obscure at the end of the boundary bank on the right. If visibility is poor a compass bearing should be followed from this last recognisable position. Exe Head (GR 751414) lies in a slight dip.

(4) From Exe Head the route follows the track heading north for 1 mile into the Chains Valley and then on to the Hoar Oak Tree (GR 747430). On reaching a point level with the tree, the walk turns right, crosses the stream and heads uphill to it. There is a gate in the wall adjacent to the tree. On passing through this gate the route now heads north along the side of open moorland, heading towards Cheriton Ridge (GR 746445).

(5) Initially this path is not obvious and again a compass bearing may be helpful if visibility is poor.

(6) After 2 miles the route leaves the moor through a field gate at Cheriton (GR 737463) and soon turns left onto a tarmac lane. Beyond Scoresdown Farm the lane becomes a track and heads steeply down the valley side to Smallcombe Bridge (GR 732470).

(7) After crossing Smallcombe Bridge, the route turns right down a path along the west bank of the river to the highway at Hillsford Bridge (GR 740477).

(8) From Hillsford Bridge the route is to the left for a short distance, following the road uphill. At the first bend on the uphill climb (GR 740479) the route turns onto a path straight ahead which leads to Myrtleberry Cleave (GR 739485), on to Lyn Cleave (GR 725490) and finally down to Lyn Bridge (GR 719485).

(9) From Lyn Bridge the route then follows a narrow lane on the opposite side of the main road which eventually becomes a tarmac path. Heading diagonally up to the north it passes the YHA Hostel and eventually reaches the centre of Lynton.

(10) As the first No. 300 Bus (summer months only) from Minehead currently does not arrive in Lynton until late morning, it is advisable to stay in Lynmouth/Lynton for at least the next two nights. There is plenty of accommodation and in addition the twin villages have a wide range of other facilities.

STAGE (8) LYNTON to LYNMOUTH VIA THE HEDDON VALLEY, 12 Miles (19 Kilometres).

This is a challenging walk. In addition to its length, there are frequent ups and downs and also many time consuming points of interest. There is no public transport but if appropriate the stage can be split into two sections by using taxis between Lynton/Lynmouth and Woody Bay.

(1) The walk starts at the centre of Lynton and heads for Lydiate Lane, a main road out of the village which initially heads westwards (GR 718493). At the point where the road doubles back uphill (GR 715492) the walk continues ahead along a narrow lane for a short distance before joining a footpath on the right (GR 714492).

(2) The path climbs to the lip of the hill, following it round to the north and then to the west before descending (GR 703491) and entering Six Acre Wood (GR 695489). The path continues, crossing a small stream and passing through Caffyns Heanton Wood to a footbridge over a second small stream (GR 692488).

(3) After crossing this footbridge the steps on the other side are followed up to a bridleway where there is a left turn heading south west to Bonhill Bridge (GR 685483) and on to Croscombe Barton, a former large farmhouse (GR 683479).

(4) From Croscombe Barton, where there is a signposted detour around the buildings, a footpath is then followed over the fields to Slattenslade (GR 677483).

(5) From Slattenslade the narrow highway is followed to the left through Martinhoe (GR 667486) and on to the footpath heading downhill to the right (GR

665482). This leads towards the Heddon Valley through Mannacott Farm (GR 662481) and on to a lane which descends to the Hunter's Inn (GR 654481). For those who might wish to cut the walk short at Slattenslade (5), a right turn on entry to the lane leads downhill to join the South West Coast Path as it proceeds eastwards along the coast road back to Lee Abbey and Lynton. Refer to item (8) onwards for the remainder of the route back to Lynton from Woody Bay.

(6) A hotel/pub, refreshments, a shop in season, a carpark and toilets are all available at the Hunter's Inn.

(7) The path starting on the right of Hunter's Inn is followed along the east bank of the River Heddon to join the South West Coast Path (GR 654490) on its way up to Highveer Point (GR 657496). For those who might wish to avoid the rather dramatic scenery of the Coast Path to the east of Heddon's Mouth, an alternative carriage route also commences on the right of the Hunter's Inn. This passes close to the Roman signalling station at the Beacon (GR 663493) before reaching the highway at the top of Woody Bay (GR 673486). From here a descent down the lane leads back to the Coast Path heading east. This carriage drive is the recommended bad weather route from the Heddon Valley to Woody Bay. A worthwhile detour to Heddon's Mouth crosses a bridge to the west bank of the river and then continues down to the sea, returning the same way.

(8) From Highveer Point the South West Coast Path is followed back to Lynton through Woody Bay (GR 675488), Lee Abbey (GR 698492) and the North Walk (GR 705497). Between Woody Bay and the start of the North Walk the route follows the public highway along the coast. The recommended detour down to the shore at Woody Bay begins next to a small dwelling where the Coast Path, recently a track, changes to a path and the track heads left down to the shore (GR 675488). The detour returns to the same point before continuing eastwards along the Coast Path. There are no facilities of any sort down at the bay.

STAGE (9) LYNMOUTH to PORLOCK, 14 Miles (23 Kilometres).

Stage (9) is is one of the longer ones with many ups and downs along the way. In addition there are several fascinating detours. With these in mind it might be better to split the stage into two with the break at County Gate. From here the No. 300 bus service (regular service during the summer months only) goes to Minehead and Porlock in one direction and Lynmouth/Lynton in the other. Apart from the optional detours. Stage (9) follows the South West Coast Path all the way to Porlock. This is well signposted, waymarked by acorn signs and also depicted on the 0. S. Outdoor Leisure Map No. 9. For this reason only the recommended detours along this section of the route are described in detail.

STAGE (9) Part One – Lynmouth to County Gate, 6 Miles (10 Kilometres).

(1) The South West Coast Path is rejoined at the footbridge over the Lyn beside the head of the harbour (GR 722495) and passes along the seaward side of the public park to the hill at the rear of the final buildings (GR 725496). From this point the route to Glenthorne is straight forward

(2) Optional detour to the site of the Roman Fort on Old Burrow Hill.

(2.1) The Coast Path leaves the path above the sea and enters the Glenthorne carriage drive at GR 793496.

(2.2) From here a right turn leads up to and past the lodge (GR 793493) where the coast path soon turns left and down into a dip. The detour to the Roman Fort follows the drive upwards for a further half mile to a field beyond a conifer plantation. This is entered through a gate (GR 790493).

(2.3) On entering the field a westerly heading is followed up to the site of the fort on the crest of the hill (GR 788493).

(2.4) The field is left by another gate onto the carriage drive (GR 787491). From here a path leads down the combe to the Sisters' Fountain (GR 792491) where the Coast Path is rejoined.

(3) Optional detour down to Glenthorne Beach.

(3.1) From the Sisters' Fountain the Coast Path is followed eastwards for a short distance. The second detour starts at a signposted track heading downhill on the left (GR 794491) which leads to Glenthorne Beach (GR 799496).

(3.2) On returning from the beach the left branch of the track is followed up Yenworthy Combe to the Pinetum where the Coast Path is rejoined (GR 802492).

(3.3) At Yenworthy Combe a left turn onto the Coast Path heads east towards Porlock. If this day's walk is planned to end at County Gate (GR 793486), a right turn should be taken from the Coast Path at Yenworthy Combe. Then on reaching a track junction (GR 799492) the track on the left leads up to the road and bus stop at County Gate.

STAGE (9) Part Two – County Gate to Porlock, 8 miles (13 Kilometres).

Part Two continues eastwards along the Coast Path. This is well signposted from Glenthorne to Porlock, including the diversion up Wheaton Combe (GR 809489) and the later diversion to Porlock.

(4) On returning by bus to County Gate (GR 793486) the Coast Path is rejoined by retracing steps down the two tracks leading to Yenworthy Combe (GR 802492).

(5) The Optional Detour to the Shingle Bank Breach near Porlock Weir.

(5.1) Starting from Porlock Weir (GR 864479) the detour follows the coast road to a point where it turns right and the shingle bank continues eastwards (GR 867476). From here the shingle bank is followed to the breach (GR 876479). Return is made the same way. No attempt should be made to cross the breach at any state of the tide.

(5.2) On return, the road (GR 867476) is followed southwards to Porlock ford (GR 867473) to join the diverted Coast Path from Porlock Weir to Porlock a mile away. The route now passes through trees at the foot of the steep hillside on the right.

(6) For those who might prefer to end the walk at Porlock Weir instead of continuing on to Porlock village, the No. 38 bus service terminates at the Weir before returning to Porlock village and Minehead.

STAGE (10) PORLOCK to MINEHEAD, 8 Miles (13 Kilometres).

The final stage of the walk begins across the lowland fields of the Vale of Porlock and then continues along the high coast back to Minehead. The first part of the stage is along the diverted South West Coast Path to Bossington. The second includes the Rugged Coast Path which should not be attempted in wild weather. Dogs are not permitted on this path. The recommended bad weather route is along the South West Coast Path to Minehead which, although exposed, only passes over undulating terrain.

(1) Starting from the church the walk proceeds east along the main street for approximately 100 yards before turning left into Sparkhayes Lane. Opposite Sparkhayes Campsite entrance there are steps heading upwards to a small bungalow estate. At its road entrance the route turns left into Villes Lane which is followed towards the sea for a quarter of a mile. At the end where the road turns to the left there is a footpath to the right of front, initially heading in the direction of the sea (GR 888473).

(2) This footpath, which has now become the diverted South West Coast Path, is followed across the fields to Bossington (GR 895480). Bossington has two tea places open in season, a car park and toilets. There are no other facilities between here and Minehead. From Bossington car park the route crosses the river and follows a bridleway which is part of the South West Coast Path. This leads to a point close to Hurlstone Point (GR 899489) where a right turn heads up steep Hurlstone Combe.

(3) At the top (GR 904487), the route leaves the South West Coast Path, turning left for a short distance up to the ridge and then downhill along it for a further short distance to join a path on the right which is not shown on the 0. S. map. At first this heads eastwards along the top of the coast before turning into East Combe where it joins the Rugged Coast Path (GR 911486).

(4) The Rugged Coast Path, is signposted but not shown on the 0.S. map. It passes through Henners Combe (GR 916488) and along a $1\frac{1}{2}$ miles of high exposed coast before coming ending at a stile beyond Grexy Combe (GR 940480).

(5) From the end of the Rugged Coast Path the way forward is straight ahead and eastwards to a path tee junction where a right turn leads up to the South

West Coast Path (GR 944477). These two sections of path, although well used, are not depicted on the 0. S. map but the Coast Path is shown.

(6) From another path junction the Coast Path turns downhill towards the sea (GR 947476) and this leads to Minehead.

(7) On the outskirts of Minehead the Coast Path becomes a lane before leading to Burgundy Road and the first houses of the town. At its end, close to the war memorial (GR 969467), the route turns downhill along Martlet Road to the town centre, the start and now the end of the walk.

POSSIBLE SHORT CUTS (For those whose time is restricted to one week or less)

Short cuts will inevitably involve some loss of pleasure. However those who only have a week or less available will have to consider them. The recommended cuts are in the eastern and western parts of the walk, leaving the central sections intact.

SHORT CUT FROM DUNSTER MARSH TO DUNSTER

(1) Following the route of Stage (1), on reaching the beach chalets at Dunster Beach (GR 997454) the modified route turns right onto a footpath beside a stream along the edge of the golf course. This soon turns left along a track up to the Old Manor (GR 995449) where it becomes a tarmac lane.

(2) Continuing along the lane there is a left turn at the next road junction and then one immediately right onto a path initially between dwellings (GR 994445) which heads up to the A39 at Loxhole Bridge (GR 995439).

(3) Directly across the busy main road, a public footpath heads across Dunster Castle Park to the car park at Dunster Steep (GR 993438) and the main road through the village.

(4) The shortened walk now follows the original Stage (3) to Horner. This modified stage is 9 miles long but most of the original Stage (1) and all the original Stage (2) have been eliminated. As a result the total length of the modified walk becomes 80 miles and the number of nights on the route are reduced by two.

SHORT CUT FROM LYNTON TO LYNMOUTH

This is a total deletion of the 12 miles long Stage (8) and there will only be one overnight stay at Lynton/Lynmouth.

The nett effect of both changes is to reduce the total length of the walk to 68 miles and the minimum time required will be less than a week.

SOME USEFUL ADDRESSES

Minehead Tourist Information Centre,
17, Friday Street,
Minehead,
West Somerset.
Tel. (01643)702624

Lynton and Lynmouth Tourist Information Centre,
Town Hall,
Lynton,
North Devon.
Tel. (01598)752225

Exmoor National Park Authority,
Exmoor House.
Dulverton,
Somerset, TA22 9HL.
Tel. (01398)323665

First Southern National Limited,
The Bus Station,
Tower Street,
Taunton,
Somerset, TAI 4AF
Tel. (01823)272033